UNENDING

HOPE

FOR THE
EXHAUSTED
ADDICT

FOREWORD BY DR WAYNE MACK

UNENDING

HOPE

FOR THE
EXHAUSTED
ADDICT

ALAN LESTER

Pleasant Word
A Division of WINEPRESS PUBLISHING

Pleasant Word (a division of WinePress Publishing, PO Box 428, Enumclaw, WA 98022) functions only as book publisher. As such, the ultimate design, content, editorial accuracy, and views expressed or implied in this work are those of the author.

Unless otherwise noted, all Scriptures are taken from the *New International Version of the Bible, the Bible Society of South Africa edition.*

ISBN 13: 978-1-4141-1204-6
ISBN 10: 1-4141-1204-1
Library of Congress Catalog Card Number: 2008901486

One imagines that a book on addiction is for someone else. As I began to read the opening words, for a flickering moment my wicked heart was ignited, but immediately convicted and at that moment I realized this book is for a heart like mine, addicted to sin.

—Kevin Lester

CONTENTS

FOREWORD

N O MATTER WHERE you travel in the world, you will find there are certain problems human beings encounter that are not limited to people of certain cultures, nationalities, economic or educational status, race, or gender. One of them is the problem of drug abuse on which this book focuses. In this book, Alan Lester helpfully describes what the person who is enslaved to drugs is experiencing; the nature and causes of drug addiction; and a biblically based practical solution to the problem. All of this will be useful to the person struggling with the problem and also to those who want to help the drug abuser to overcome the problem. Much of what is written in this tome is addressed to the person struggling with the drug-abuse issue. Hence, you will frequently find the author using the word "you." So this is the kind of book that a person who is addicted to drugs should carefully read. Nevertheless, the information found in this volume will be equally valuable for anyone who wants to be more effective in helping people to put off their enslavement to drugs.

The approach Alan Lester explains and recommends in this book is not merely a behavioristic, moralistic, or simplistic approach. He gives insights and perspectives that go to the root of the problem in a thoroughly biblical and very practical way. One of the things that make this book unique is the fact that the perspectives on drug abuse presented in it are in keeping with a biblical anthropology. As you read through this volume, you will find solid material that exposes the inaccuracy of the very popular concept that alcoholism and drug abuse are genetic in origin or that they are to be regarded as a disease. Furthermore, since accurately defining a problem is essential for solving a problem, Alan presents a clear, convincing, and accurate biblical definition of the true nature of drug abuse. Another valuable factor provided by this book for dealing successfully with the problem of drug abuse is having an understanding of the characteristics of the person who is most likely to become enslaved to this kind of addiction.

One of the caricatures that is often given to those who reject the popular ideas about drug abuse and insist on using a biblical approach is that all they do is call it a sin and, therefore, give very superficial and unhelpful counsel. Anyone who will carefully read this book will understand that effectively promoting biblical change involves much more than that. They will be encouraged to facilitate what I call in the biblical counselling courses I teach the key elements of the biblical counselling process. The material found in this manuscript will emphasize and illustrate factors that will provide hope for change, the importance of gathering sufficient information about the person, and properly interpreting what the data indicates about the person and his problem. It will also clarify the kinds of instruction a drug abuser needs and the kind of commitment he must make. It will also give many valuable strategies and practical ideas for putting off the enslavement to drugs and putting on a new pattern of freedom and godly living.

I commend Alan Lester for providing the material found in this volume on what has become and is becoming, even more so, a very common and destructive problem. I am grateful that throughout this book he has manifested an unswerving confidence and unshakable trust in the practical reliability and sufficiency of God's Word. In this manuscript your attention will be redirected away from the failed and flawed human solutions to the infallible Word of God. It does not float one more theory in an endless barrage of theories on how to solve the problem of drug addiction. Rather, it points to the certainty of God's eternal truth as the absolute basis by which to live and succeed.

—Dr. Wayne Mack
Professor of Biblical Counselling
Grace School of Ministry in Pretoria, South Africa
Professor of Biblical Counselling
Expositor's Seminary in Little Rock, Arkansas
Member of the Academy of the National
Association of Nouthetic Counsellors

INTRODUCTION AND ACKNOWLEDGMENTS

IN THIS BOOK you will not find lofty words but a personal appeal from my heart. Its substance has been brewed in the furnace of temptation to sin and the struggle toward personal purity. The words are direct, without euphemism, and they are designed specifically for those who are truly exhausted in their addiction—as the title suggests. I have worked hard to make this book gripping and realistic and to deal with issues that many are too fearful to admit are in their hearts.

Read carefully and you will discover many confessions I have made in an attempt to demonstrate solidarity with you as you struggle. I write absolutely convinced that there truly is hope for you, even though you are too tired to fight any more. In fact, the more exhausted you are with your sin, the more hope I see for you. In this book you will discover how it is that you can be so trapped by things you know are wrong. You will be challenged to deal with them as you read. You will be exposed to a world-view that is far greater than that of your present slavery. In this book you will find real hope, God's hope, God's unending hope for you, exhausted addict.

I owe the greatest debt of gratitude to Dr. Edward T. Welch for his book, *Addictions: A Banquet in the Grave*. Dr. Welch has surpassed my expectations in his understanding of addictions. I have used his book as a textbook for addicts under my care, and it has proved to be an invaluable source of wisdom. All who read this book and Dr. Welch's book will notice his influence in my material. While I lean heavily on Dr. Welch's material, I don't imply that I have any personal relationship with him or that he would even agree with what I write.

I would also like to thank Dr. Wayne Mack for his kind readiness to read my manuscript and write a foreword. This expression of confidence and his highly valued friendship have given me great motivation in the writing of this material.

I am also grateful to others who have read through my work making valuable comments and suggesting modifications. My mother, Jill Lester, waded through the first draft and suggested modifications on almost every page. Thank you! My brother, Kevin, read it and encouraged me immensely by grasping the exact import of what I am saying in this book. Thank you! My brother in Christ, Pieter Swart, encouraged me continually by his enthusiasm and honest comments not only on the initial draft but on the edited version as well. Pieter also put his heart into the work he did on the cover design. Thank you! David Wade put significant effort into the cover and author photographs in his studio. Thank you! Others have encouraged me in the writing of this book, including my dear wife, Charleen, and my father, Clinton Lester. Thank you all!

To my brother-in-law and sister, Shaun and Jean Schutte, I am grateful for the financial resources necessary to publish this book. I receive this blessing as from the hand of the Lord.

May the God who has saved me by His grace and who drives me on toward personal holiness, so work in your life that you will be rescued from sin and its consequences and will surge ahead in the Christian life delighting in your blessed Savior, for His glory!

Chapter 1

YOU ARE BIASED

CANDI COULD FEEL the blood rushing to her face, her whole body pulsating in the alarm of the moment. She just wanted to die as she heard the sounds of her own voice blaring from the DVD playing on the home theatre in the sitting room. If it had been a cute, little home movie that had her parents rapt attention, she would have joined them and soaked up the adoration. They were stunned—their reactions not yet solidified.

A ghastly chain of calamities had unfolded minutes before as she had looked out of her bedroom window and seen her ex-boyfriend striding toward the front door with a package in his hand. She had heard his teenage voice making a hurried explanation and some short words of thanks from her father. He had then slipped away on his bicycle down the road.

Curious, and a little concerned about the package, Candi had made her way to the sitting room to enquire when she heard the sounds of a young woman engaged in a sexual encounter emitting from the room. The voice was hers!

In that instant, she wanted to die. Her parents had been so good to her, and she had brutally disappointed them. She could almost see her father through the wall, staring aghast, as she tried to melt away without drawing attention to the fact that she had almost barged straight into this volatile moment. With her cheeks blazing hot and a deathly feeling in her belly, she rushed for her bedroom, locked the door, and smothered her tears in her pillow.

She was dreading the moment of seeing her dear mom's face again. How could she live under this roof any longer with her father? Her life had come to an end, and there seemed to be only one thing left to do. She would kill herself.

How could she have done so much damage? How had she ended up like this? Sadly, in a society that feeds on the milk of sexual suggestions in every form of media, sexual experimentation comes to be an expected norm rather than taboo. Candi had gotten into this exciting new way of life quite easily. After making close friends with some girls at school and spending a lot of time with them, she was drawn into the vortex.

In her parents' day same-gender relationships were unheard of, but after her first experience, Candi could think of nothing else. Driven by a growing yearning, she pursued this new relationship until it had become a normal part of her life. It was comforting, exciting, and deeply emotional.

She found that her hunger for this kind of intimacy began to overflow the boundaries of her present relationship, and she began to dapple in other types of relationships. Before long, she was swallowed up in a dark world of perverted parties.

Something that shocked her at first was when one of the guys she had been with persuaded her to try a little coke. The rush was beyond anything she had ever experienced, and she began to see everyone around her with new eyes. They were just so beautiful. The urge to melt into the sensual experiences of this world was overwhelming, and she gave herself away.

Before that particular evening was over, she began to feel depressed. Having made her way home, she slipped into bed and lay there for hours, unable to sleep. The great feeling she had experienced earlier was gone, and now she just felt cheap and used. It had all felt so appealing until now. Nothing was clean or pure anymore. She began to weep, sobbing into her pillow until she had no strength left to cry.

If only this was the end of the story, she may have escaped most of the misery that lay ahead. In spite of the misery she had endured the night before, a new longing began to build up within her. She had to have more coke. She had to recapture that awesome plateau she had reached the night before. Skipping breakfast the next morning and, then, school, she found her friend at home and urged her to go back with her to the club.

As the music pulsated that night and the inhibitions were eased away by drug-induced euphoria, Candi again stole the event. So engaged, she didn't even mind the fact that someone was filming her. She couldn't conceive that anyone would watch this and not be blown away by the sheer beauty of it all. She was giving away the most delightful side of her self and wanted everyone to have a share.

As she sat on the edge of her friend's sofa the next morning with her head between her hands, the video recording was concerning her. Her friend was doing her best to persuade her that they would both be rich. All her other friends were doing it, posting videos like that of themselves on the internet, and they were just raking in the cash. "Your parents will never find out," she urged. "They never use the internet. Anyway, even if they did, they would never go to a site where you download this kind of stuff."

Candi was feeling relentlessly irritable inside her creepy skin, constantly plagued by her wretched running nose and persistently bunged up sinuses. All this drove her to get more. She couldn't wait for the next snort. This had become her life. She couldn't imagine existence without the romance of her lovers or her beloved powder.

With time, a nagging concern began to grow beside the moans of her tearful conscience. What was bothering her now was the cost of her stuff. Her adoring suppliers had gradually withdrawn from her as new girls had come to absorb their adoration. Exhausted, but driven to desperation, selling the videos of herself with her friend and with the others seemed to be the only way to make the money she needed without being busted. After all, the internet is so huge, what chance is there that anyone who knew her would recognise her?

The last thing she bargained on was her ex-boyfriend showing up at the door with that DVD. After the shock of exposure, she sat in a session with a family therapist while in rehab plagued by the way she had spiralled into moral filth. She said to the therapist, "I hate myself. How could I get involved with this smut? I thought I was so cool... My life feels as if it's over. I hate what I have done to my parents, the disappointment and the hurt. When they got a DVD that my ex-boyfriend dropped off at the house... I felt like killing myself. I feel so ashamed and don't want to hurt anyone anymore."[1]

Something was driving Candi down into the dungeons of sin, and I don't believe I have to describe her cravings in any more detail because you know what I'm speaking about. You know the kind of desires in your heart that draw you, like gravity, toward the things you are ashamed to admit to being in love with. There are desires in your heart that you will never dare utter to another living soul. You feel they simply couldn't take it.

This opens up a monstrous question today. Why would a beautiful young girl like Candi, who grew up in a respectable home under good parents, with everything going for her, succumb to the yearning for elicit encounters? Unfortunately, there are many in the queue, all jabbering answers to this question. Some of them are saying that you have left your good, stable home behind in order to pursue a life of licentiousness because you are curious, or because of peer-pressure, or because of lack of family values, or because you have no idea of boundaries, or because society has neglected to look into proper values, or because you were given too much pocket money.[2]

For sure, these may all be secondary factors in your strong desire for immoral living, but they are not the primary cause.

But, there is more. Not only are you aware of these hankerings in your heart to indulge yourself in things that appeal to your most fleshly lusts, you also know that to long for and engage in those activities is wrong. You couldn't convince yourself or anyone else that you truly believed that when you mugged that man on the pavement and took his money to buy a shot of smack, that you were doing what was right. Of all the arguments you may conjure up, you must confess that there is a niggling sense deep inside of you that you are not doing something noble, good, proper, commendable (Romans 2:15). Even though

Candi pursued her perverted sex life with such eagerness, isn't her sickening sense of guilt when she was caught a declaration that she knew what she was doing was wrong? Isn't that same horrible feeling you experience at the thought of getting caught a declaration that what you are doing is wrong?

Yes, I agree that most people would be shocked if you had to blatantly divulge the secret recesses of your heart—the same would be true of me. I find comfort, however, in the fact that this sense of longing for sin, regardless of its consequences, is by no means something new. In fact, this yearning capacity and action of your heart has been documented millennia back in history. Your deepest, most hidden lusts are common knowledge to God. In fact, He has described what He sees when He looks into the fallen human heart.

> The LORD saw how great man's wickedness on earth had become, and that every inclination of the thoughts of his heart was only evil all the time.
>
> —Genesis 6:5

When God looks at your heart, He doesn't have to wonder whether you became a heroin addict because you had too much pocket money. No! He sees that there is a bias in your heart. There is a longing, a hankering, a gravitational pull inside of you so that you are always prone to do what is wrong rather than what is right. It is no wonder you indulge in the sin that grabs you most when the opportunity presents itself. This, says God, is what comes most naturally to fallen man.

That is not the only time God says that. God Himself called out, "Oh, that their hearts would be inclined to fear me and keep all my commands always, so that it might go well with them and their children forever." (Deuteronomy 5:29).[3] What would thrill God more than anything else about humanity would be to find a person who truly desires to do what pleases Him. If you are hearing what God is saying here, you will hear Him declaring that the trend He sees in fallen human beings is that their hearts are straining toward something other than God. And when Scripture speaks of the heart it is referring to your inner person. It is speaking about the place where you think and plan and desire.[4] Has it struck you yet that the basic reason you do what you do is because you have an unexplainable yearning in your heart to do what is wrong rather than what is right?

God knows what you are "disposed to do" even before you do it (Deuteronomy 31:21). Do you think it is a great secret that your inner life is constantly filled with thoughts of sexual gratification, gaining intimate access to another man's wife or another woman's husband, deceiving other people so they don't know what you are really like, doing things and saying things so that other people don't get an advantage rather than you, having an unquenchable desire to have more, doing foolish and wrong things simply because you have a desire and that desire must be met? (See See Mark 7:21-23) Do you think that if you simply don't tell someone that you have a secret drinking habit that no-one will know what kind of material you are really made of? No. God has laid all of the material of which your and my hearts are made out in the open.

Not only do you have a hellish bent toward perversion, but your heart, says God, is also positively hostile toward Him (See Romans 8:7). In the same way that water resists mixing with oil, so you can't stand the thought of being too closely involved with God. His standards are unrealistic to you. They prohibit you from doing the things that your heart longs for the most. You feel uncomfortable at the mention of God's name and are even having second thoughts about reading this book because it has started talking more about God than it is talking about the story with which it opened. What God requires of you is to simply say, "Yes Lord, that's true. I am like that." God requires you to say the same thing in your heart about yourself as He is saying about you in the Bible.

Sadly, masses of addicts are wasted, not in the way that addicts prattle the term, but are wasted, or ruined, forever. They are wasted because they refuse to love the truth and so be saved (See 2 Thessalonians 2:10). They push forward, just a little longer, just a little deeper, just another shot, another joint—until they are swallowed up into eternal misery. The woman who wrote the article about Candi spoke about the young people she works with. She said that she is shocked again and again by their lack of remorse.

> The child looked at me with blank eyes and a lifeless expression. She told me that she does not think there is anything wrong with what they are doing. When the results on her pregnancy test and HIV and STI screening returned, they were clear, and she said sarcastically; "See, I told you that everything is fine. I can look after myself."[5]

Yearning for gratification, they will hunt down their lusts regardless of the danger of sexually transmitted diseases, regardless of the disgrace of getting caught, regardless of the fact that they are abusing and disgracing their families, regardless of whether it is right or wrong, regardless of the law of the land, regardless of what God desires. Yes, these things may enter your mind as you feel the prick of yet another needle, but as long as you are feeling that rush again, all of these things fade into oblivion. Thinking about the morality of what you are doing seems laughable (See Proverbs 14:9).

You may think that I am being unusually harsh with you as an addict, but I am not. The fact is that this same inclination is in the heart of every living person. Every person who has ever lived has lived his whole life with this cursed longing for his lusts. Paul tells us this when he says,

> There is no one righteous, not even one; there is no one who understands, no one who seeks God. All have turned away, they have together become worthless; there is no one who does good, not even one.
>
> —Romans 3:10-12

Every living person longs for the wrong things. Even though Candi grew up in such a good home, she discovered that there is a coarse longing in her heart for what is wrong. She was biased. As an addict, you have discovered that there is that same yearning in your heart. You are biased. I am biased. What are you biased toward? What is it that you long for more than you hunger for God? What do you consider the most wonderful thing you can experience in this world? What is your greatest dream? Answer these questions, and you will know what you are biased toward. You will have simultaneously answered the question, "What or whom are you worshipping?" May God grant you a brand new yearning to be at peace with God and to be like the Lord Jesus forever.

Chapter 2

WHAT FLAVOR IS
YOUR DESIRE?

WHAT FLAVOR IS your desire? In this chapter I would like to define exactly what I am speaking about when I use the term addict, or addiction. It would be dangerous for me to assume that you and I are thinking of the same thing when we use those terms. I would like to pull out all of the stuffing you may have packed into that word and fill it with the stuffing the Bible provides when it speaks about what is commonly known as addictions.

To begin with, notice that people who are described as addicts are people whose desires have dragged them to things that make their desires obvious. It is easier to spot a person who can't stay away from alcohol than it is a person who can't stay away from pornography. The one is more public while the other is more secret. Why is it then that we call one an addict and the other escapes the label? Surely it has to do with how visible his struggles with his desires are and how dramatically his habits affect his life and the lives of the people around him.

A consideration of some different "addictions" will be helpful here.

It is very seldom that people become addicted to things like tissue salts, vitamin C, or foot-powder. Why? Simply because they provide no pleasant sensory experience. It is an absurd suggestion that someone would become addicted to vitamin K because of the rush he experienced when over a period of three years he noticed a slightly healthier appearance to his fingernails. No, the world has become besotted with things that give you a rush; things that add excitement and zest to life; things that break the painful ordinariness of daily routine. What I am saying in this book is that when you come under the control of something you do repeatedly in order to satisfy your desire for a pleasant sensory experience that you are addicted. This is how I have defined the term addicted. I would like to show that this is how the Bible defines this trend that we have come to know as addictions, in our day.

You would think that if addictions are such a prevalent phenomenon in our world, the Bible would have something to say about it, and it certainly does. The Bible speaks about these things because God understands this longing in the fallen human heart. When speaking about addictions, you will find some themes in Scripture that are prominent—they are sleep, food, sex, and alcohol. All of these are major areas of life in which you and I can become entangled in controlling sin.

The Bible shows how some people long to eat more food than they should because it tastes nice and gives them a satisfied feeling. For some people, food is everything. Food is their comforter and companion through the harsh realities of life. Two examples of this from the Bible are "The Rich Fool" (Luke 12:13-21) and the rich man in Jesus' "Parable of the Rich

Man and Lazarus" (Luke 16:19-31). Consider also how Paul contrasts people whose God is their stomach and whose minds are on earthly things with people whose citizenship is in heaven (Philippians 3:19-20).[6]

Some people can think of nothing else to do but enjoy the relaxed atmosphere of sleeping. Pop a few pills and drift away from reality into restful sleep. For some people, sleep is their lust. A classic proverb that encapsulates this teaching is Proverbs 6:9-11. There a lazy person is seen slowly drifting into sleep, but being suddenly attacked by poverty which is pictured as an armed assailant. Proverbs 20:13 warns of the danger of falling in love with sleep.

The Bible also speaks about alcohol. Proverbs 23:19-25 is an outstanding passage of Scripture that teaches on the attractiveness of alcohol and the misery of those who are enticed and captured by its sparkle in the glass. I need not speak more at this point on the attraction of alcohol as a mind-altering substance. It certainly breaks the monotony of the daily grind. It certainly provides that pleasant sensory experience.

The Bible also speaks about sex. Just as sin has spoiled everything in God's creation, it has spoiled sex, too. After the fall, men and women began to eye each other deviously as sex objects (Genesis 3:7-10).[7] The craving to rudely abuse the good feature of the sexual desire God has built into human beings can seem unbearable until that craving is gratified—as in Candi's story. The Bible sees the urge to gratify sexual desire in a sinful way—as a part of the sinful nature of every human being (Colossians 3:5).

It must be pointed out that while sexual relations between a married man and woman are right and pure (1 Corinthians 7:1-6), even that sexual relationship can be pursued to the point where you can be acting sinfully. You can become so obsessed with sexual satisfaction even within a marriage relationship that you can be controlled by that urge. So satisfaction in sexual encounters is another example of a pleasant sensory experience.

Edward Welch suggests a number of other things that bring this pleasant sensory experience. I have modified the list slightly to suggest the following things you could look for in your personal desires.[8]

Maybe you love the thrill of getting angry. You love the sense of power that surges through you when you feel you are compelled to exert your authority. People shy away from you as you blow your top like a volcano. No-one dares utter a word because they fear the fury you may direct toward them. If you regularly get angry, you will know how this habit transforms you, lifting you from the mundane, monotonous tones of a regular day, and putting you high on an untouchable plateau from which you command your will. Anger, you will agree, provides you with a pleasant sensory experience.

You may prefer the pleasant sensory experience you receive from receiving or giving affection. Unless you have heard kind, encouraging words or received a gentle caress from someone, you feel you can't bring yourself to perform at your peak. You feel you need that soft, tender touch in order to live a full, meaningful day.

For you it may be weightlifting. You warm up in the gym and pump iron until your body begins to glisten with sweat. You push it more and more until you begin to feel that consuming euphoria that comes from pushing yourself to the limit. You take note of your beautifully shaped physique in the mirror and find yourself driven by the good feelings in your mind and body—the pleasant sensory experience. You are filled with a sense of well-being.

It could also be nicotine. You cannot imagine getting through this day, this morning, this hour, this minute without the pleasant sensory experience of drawing deep on a cigarette. After a few drags, the moments standing before you appear more manageable and easy to endure. I have found this compulsion more difficult for an addict to break than any other, except maybe the craving for heroin.

You may find yourself immobile for hours every day watching television. The stimulation flowing from the tube into your imagination takes you away into another world, making the stark realities of ordinary life more bearable. You come to know the characters in your favorite shows as real people. Maybe you even come to view yourself as someone like your favorite characters. You are drawn into a fabricated world where you experience life through the eyes of posers. You experience the pleasant sensory experiences that are brought on by the emotional tones of the narrative flashing before your glassy eyes. You feel their pain. You identify with them. You glory in their triumph and experience their longing for revenge.

It could be the sound of tinkling coins falling into the stainless steel trough of a slot machine; the thrill of drawing that lever, anticipating the possibility of your life changing forever; slipping your chips across the soft green felt; watching the little roulette ball dance across the numbers, searching for your jackpot. The pleasant sensory experience you feel as the moment bursts upon you, and you have won.

How about the calm sense of confidence in which you are decorated after the initial bodily sensation of a coke rush? You are unquestionably intelligent, beautiful, and completely unable to make a fool of yourself or flake out in the middle of an engaging evening or business meeting. Nothing slips your notice and you are able to interpret all of your surroundings in a unique way—running circles around the mere men in your social circle.

Or the intense thrill of bursting through the tapes at the end of the twelve hundred metre track event. You are a finely tuned machine, and you are untouchable. Men admire your power; women desire you. If only they were you, but they are not. It is you who commands that respect because of the agony you have put into your training. You have earned this victory, and the athletes who came behind you have faded into insignificance, they don't quite measure up. What a pleasant sensory experience comes over you as the crowds roar in ecstasy.

Could your pleasant sensory experience come from the thrill of being the life-of-the-party, telling stories about yourself that have everyone around you mesmerised? The ordinary people, inexperienced fools in your eyes, drink in the tales of your exciting lifestyle, wishing it was them having the stunning girls and trendy guys worship them. In order to keep this admiration flowing, however, you find it necessary to add some anabolic steroids to your weedy experiences. No-one will ever know you're not a real hero.

Ordinarily people think you are a placid, peaceful man, content with your family life and standard job. Unbeknown to them, you spend hours chasing the fantasy of internet porn. You are able to show your face at church services and find your romantic, pleasant sensory experience thrills with the racy babes on the net. Compared to them, you find the Bible and God insipid, yet you are not ready to be known as a lusting heathen. You like the atmosphere among church people, the way they accept you and are too fearful to ask you how your devotional life is.

We could really go on to a long list of things that bring pleasant sensory experiences. Others are sugar, shoplifting, heroin, chocolate, risk, success, winning, ecstasy, clubbing, comfort, riches, eating out, movies, coffee breaks, computer games, etc. Take a moment to consider what it is in your life that you use to bring you your pleasant sensory experiences.

It may even be a combination of any number of these things. You pursue those habits and activities or thought patterns because they provide you with an experience that you consider pleasant. They feed your fantasies and thereby provide you with an immediate thrill by means of the information and substances you permit to enter your mind and body through your physical senses—your eyesight, your hearing, your senses of taste, touch, and smell.

Everyone does this to some degree. In most people's lives these trends are quite unnoticeable, but in the life of a person we would generally call an addict, his devotion to a particular substance has become noticeable because of the way it affects him and the way he demands more at any cost. Have you noticed anything yet that you do simply because you like the feeling? Have you noticed how you do certain things, go to certain places, speak to certain people, eat certain foods because of the way they make you feel? The things that make you feel better, you do more often. The things that produce unpleasant feelings, you do less often. So I say again, it is the position of this book, that when you are controlled by your desire to do something that gives you a pleasant sensory experience, you are addicted.

Moving one step forward, there is an obvious question that begs to be answered. "What's wrong with doing things that make me feel good?" The answer to this question raises a critical distinction. First, understand that many things that make you feel good are not wrong in themselves. Take a nice hot cup of coffee on a cold day for example. There is nothing wrong with that. Consider the great feeling you experience after a good workout. There's nothing wrong with that. There's also nothing wrong with the sense of well-being you get from helping someone else who is in difficulty.

So if there is nothing wrong with enjoying some pleasant sensory experiences, what is the problem with any pleasant sensory experience? Why can't I smoke my joint in the evening? I'm not hurting anyone, am I? Why can't I watch porn secretly? It's only me that's affected? These are the kinds of arguments that begin to grow like warts on the mind of a person who is bent on satisfying himself.

The truth is shocking and needs to be considered seriously. For a start, some of the things we have mentioned above are sinful because they are described as sin in Scripture, but there is another point of distinction I would like to make. Has it ever struck you that there is a definite connection between your pleasant sensory experiences and your devotion to the Lord? This is a war. Pleasant sensory experiences are waging war against your devotion to Christ. You may suppose I am being absurd, "How can a cup of coffee fight against my desire for Christ?"

Consider for a moment what the Lord is saying in Deuteronomy 31:20. The Lord is speaking about the time when Israel, who had been wandering around in the desert for forty years, would eventually come into the great new Promised Land. In complete contrast to the harsh desert conditions they were used to, in the Promised Land they would have houses to live in rather than tents. They would have established fruit trees and vines they didn't plant. They would not be constantly packing up their things and moving to place after place after place ad nauseam. Life would rapidly become more comfortable.

The Lord speaks about this comfort. He says,

> When I have brought them into the land flowing with milk and honey, the land I promised on oath to their forefathers, and when they eat their fill and thrive, they will turn to other gods and worship them, rejecting me and breaking my covenant.
>
> —Deuteronomy 31:20

You see, God understands what fallen human beings are like. We like things that look good, smell good, taste good, feel good, and sound good to such a degree that we will even choose those pleasant sensory experiences over the experience of true communion with the living God! There is a definite connection here between your pleasant sensory experiences and your devotion to God. Do you think it is possible that your relationship with the Lord has never thrived because you are more devoted to pleasant sensory experiences than you are to Him?

There is another text that thuds a doleful tone in this neighborhood. The Lord is speaking to Israel in Hosea 13:5-6. There He says,

I cared for you in the desert, in the land of burning heat. When I fed them, they were satisfied; when they were satisfied, they became proud; then they forgot me.

Can you hear the queasy impact as these people who should have loved God with all of their hearts, eat the good food out of His hand, and immediately fall into the godlessness of being ruled by pleasant sensory experiences?

The pleasant experiences you enjoy in your life, whether sleeping in a warm bed, chatting on the phone, drinking a cold drink on a hot day, or seeing beautiful things, have an impact on your devotion to God, whether you admit it or not. They impact your attitude toward God. God says so.

To make a confession, there are not many Christians who would deny there are many mornings they struggle to get out of bed to have a time of communion with the Lord before they begin their day. I can appreciate that struggle. So before we have even slipped out of bed in the morning, pleasant sensory experience is interfering with your devotion to the Lord. Will you simply lie in bed and utter some silent prayers to the Lord, or will you get up, pour out your heart to the Lord in prayer, feast on His Word, and go out into your day with the readiness that comes from being committed to living this day for the glory of the Lord?

Regardless of whether you got up early or not, what is the next thing you do in the morning? For some, the first cup of coffee is mandatory before they can function. Coffee is warm. It has a full, pleasant, homely aroma and flavor. It also gives you just enough lift to get you launched into the next activity of the day. Here again, you are enjoying a pleasant sensory experience. What's less noticeable, but should now become more obvious, is that you have glided straight from one pleasant sensory experience to another. The gap between the two is so small that you restrict your negative sensory experience to a minimum.

You may then take a shower or bath, with the temperature the way you like it, another pleasant sensory experience. Sit in a chair where you are comfortable to read your Bible and pray for as long as you consider necessary. Rarely will a less-than-desperate person engage in these activities for longer than they are comfortable. You eat the breakfast of your choice, you run your eyes over your favorite newspaper or the cover of a magazine with a lovely picture on the front—all pleasant sensory experiences.

You slip into your car and adjust the air temperature and the music in order to make your journey pleasant. You may ride a bicycle to work in order to save some cash, and there you undergo some negative sensory experience. Yet, when you arrive at work your metabolism is rushing, and you have a good sense of well-being.

Arriving at the office, you make yourself as comfortable as you can in your work and expose yourself to as little inconvenience and discomfort as possible. There are coffee breaks, pleasant conversations, sunny offices on a winter's day—every little detail that you gather around you to make work more bearable. Whatever you do, wherever you go in life, you are confronted with these pleasant and unpleasant sensory experiences. Because few of us like to be freezing cold, melting hot, exhausted, or hungry, we arrange our lives in such a way that we enjoy as many pleasant sensory experiences as possible in our day.

Take note. You don't even notice that you are driven or motivated by these pleasant sensory experiences in your daily routine. I can't say there is anything wrong with that cup of coffee. Yet, I can say that there is something wrong with a life that is a chain of pleasant sensory experiences. It is that kind of life that has no room for God. As you move from one pleasant sensory experience to the next, no convenient place is found in your chain for devotion to the Lord because devotion to the Lord is a discipline that cannot always be classed as a pleasant sensory experience. Often it is hard to pray, hard to read the Bible, hard to study, hard to memorize, hard to evangelize, and hard to focus your mind on Christ and His agenda in His world rather than on what brings you a sense of physical enjoyment.

You may be caught up in a chain such as this without even being aware of it. So here is the acid test. Is there space in your chain for devotion to Christ? When you must wake up on a cold morning to spend time in the Word and prayer, does your desire to continue to sleep or your desire to delight the heart of God win the battle? When you are dreaming about your wedding, your new car, your overseas holiday, or winning the lottery, are you able to stop daydreaming and occupying your mind with things that bring you pleasant sensory experiences and set your mind on Christ? The question is this: Can you say no to pleasant sensory experiences when the time has come to devote yourself to God's desires rather than your own?

I challenge you, as you live an ordinary life, to try saying "No!" to some of the pleasant sensory experiences you relish the most. Try getting up a little earlier for devotions. Try memorising Scripture. Try speaking to someone else about Christ. Try sacrificing your favorite TV program to spend time with your family with an open Bible. Can you say no? Is pleasant sensory experience or devotion to God winning the battle in your life?

Is this the struggle you are familiar with? Typically, if you have given yourself over to your yearning for pleasant sensory experiences to the degree where everyone has noticed your habits, you have probably been labelled an addict.

So there is a critical connection between your desires for pleasant sensory experiences and your devotion to the Lord. Who would have said that a chain of such seemingly insignificant things could be restraining you with such power from the blessings of God? Oh, you've tried to break free, but just can't.

Chapter 3

YOU HAVE
EVERYTHING YOU NEED

WHAT FRIGHTENS ME and should frighten you about this strong chain of pleasant sensory experiences is that if you are living like that, you are not safe! Tangled in her own chain, Candi was not safe, and neither are you. In one distressing sentence, God reveals the most secret thoughts of a person bound by this chain. He thinks, I will be safe, even though I persist in going my own way. Regardless of whether you have deliberately calculated your chances of being safe, while washing down your final ecstasy with a swig of Coke or not, is irrelevant. The fact that you are doing it is a demonstration of the fact that you believe you will be safe. You have deceived yourself into thinking that you can actually do this, enjoy the rave and live to do it again. God says this is what you are thinking, *I will be safe, even though I persist in going my own way* (Deuteronomy 29:19).[9]

Even more shocking is the truth that it is the person who thinks in this way who is simultaneously the person who is turning away from the living God (Deuteronomy 29:18). Is not your conscience alive as you read this terrible warning to the person whose heart turns away from the living God? Are you not painfully aware that you are persisting in going your own way in spite of the fact that you know that your lifestyle of pursuing pleasant sensory experiences rather than God is wrong? Is your heart not screaming within you as you prepare to brush these words aside? Do you realize, dear friend, that you are persisting in going your own way in opposition to God?

To live in opposition to God is a dreadful thing because God says in that same portion of Scripture that He will single such people out for disaster. You are not safe! While you expend all your energy softening your experience of life with the things that thrill you the most, do you not see that you are earning for yourself instead the most unspeakable horrors?

To you, my dear friend, reading this page, whose life has not fallen into the misery of full addiction, let me say this. You may have managed to restrict your compulsion to play computer games or spend time in internet chat rooms, but you still have the same core principle operating in your heart that drives the full-blown, miserable addict. What has held you back from the free-fall into that wretchedness is not your own ingenuity but the gracious restraining hand of God. Don't go and admire the person who looks back at you in the mirror, admire, thank, and praise God for His mercy to you personally.

Seeing you mulling over these thoughts drives me to shout out a word of hope. You have stopped to think about your life. You have said, "Yes, I do experience these cravings, yearnings, and longings for pleasant sensory experiences, and I have not been able to master them. I have managed to momentarily break the power of one, but another immediately takes its place." I see your losing hope that there really is a solution to your struggle. For that reason, I want to unveil before your eyes the wonderful fact that regardless of your personal experience of failure, God is the God of the exhausted addict. He sees hope for you. God has provided the equipment you need to come out of the danger and misery of your addiction.

In the newspaper article from which I constructed Candi's story, the therapist suggested a number of solutions to people in that same situation. She suggested that parents talk to their teenagers about boundaries with behaviour experimentation and to give them guidance on healthy and functional behaviour. She suggested that parents keep communication channels open with their children—that they explain the negative impact risky behaviour will have on them in later life.

As you struggle with the cravings that are driving you to despair, allow me to ask you one question, "Would those solutions do it for you?" Surely you have heard these things before—bland, powerless psychological jargon, the arms of which are helpless to reach to the core of your struggles. These solutions are impotent. What you need is someone who fully grasps that you're in a hellish brawl with your lusts and you are losing the war.

The problem is that the world is a zoo of voices, a different one calling from every camp, all conflicting. Which one do you trust? Who can you listen to? Is there any reason you should even be reading this book? There is also a story of a man who went to a psychologist because he had cultivated a hostile relationship with his father. His father had died, yet the man was still seething against him even in his grave. Following his therapist's advice, he went and urinated on his father's grave.

Instead of feeling better, the man now felt far worse because of what he'd done. Obviously, you can't simply trust any advice thrown your way.

What further complicates your predicament is that you must do something about these urges in your heart. You long for pleasant sensory experiences, engage in them, and reap the ensuing miserable consequences. You are wedged in a trap from which you cannot escape. The longings are real. The actions are real. The consequences are real. You must do something. If you didn't really believe that, you wouldn't be reading this page. Please follow me to discover the fact that God really does have a delightful solution to your personal struggles.

By now, it should have become clear that the deepest longings in your heart have been perfectly described in the Scriptures to which we have referred. You do experience a craving in your heart. You are drawn to things that give you a pleasant sensory experience. You do demonstrate by doing those things that you feel safe to do them. Unfortunately, you do often reap the negative consequences of that pursuit and regardless of the consequences of which you are now aware, the eternal consequences of sin swarm above your head. It is God who has described the yearnings in your heart. The God who made you and who completely understands the ghoulish death-struggle in which you are ensnared. The God who completely understands the most secret recesses of your heart also spreads before you the only radically transforming solution in His universe.

Many men from South Africa have, over recent years, been accepting contracts to work in Iraq as security personnel. Because the pay far exceeds what they could earn in their home country, they risk their lives in order to redeem their families from debt and poverty.

Imagine for a moment you had applied for such a contract. You respond to a phone call to attend an interview in which you are accepted as a suitable candidate. You are immediately issued with body armor and other military kit. Before you leave the office, your new employer advances you a sum of money from your first salary check and instructs you to go and buy everything you will need personally because you are going to be posted in a very remote place. What would you go buy?

As your list gets longer and longer—toothpaste, deodorant, spare shoelaces, writing paper, spare pen, etc.—you keep remembering other things—headache tablets, emergency toilet paper, razor, towel, etc. The time comes for you to pack your bag and to leave for the airport. As you pack your bag, you become more and more aware of your vulnerability. Do you have everything you will need?

Suppose you arrive at your remote camp and are standing in the queue for your first evening meal. You are far from home as you gingerly edge your teeth into your first camel steak, and instantly remember one thing you forgot to buy—nausea tablets! You don't have everything you need.

The Bible is not like that. God, who does not lie (See 1 Samuel 15:29, Titus 1:2), declares that He has given you everything you need in the bloody onslaught you are facing. Let's spend a moment considering this fact.

In 2 Peter 1:3, God says that "His divine power has given us everything we need for life and godliness through our knowledge of Him who called us by His own glory and goodness." God has made resources available to you in which you will find everything you need in any situation. These resources include the things God has said—the Bible, and the empowering presence of His Holy Spirit. There is one restriction though. You may have noticed it in the verse. These resources are available to people who have been called by God. Peter is writing to people who are believers in the Lord Jesus Christ in the same way that he is a believer in the Lord Jesus Christ (2 Peter 1:1). He is speaking to people whom God has saved by His grace.

God also bursts the same truth out before our longing eyes in 2 Timothy 3:16-17. *Because* all Scripture is breathed out by God, its words are so powerful and useful that they are the *only* words in God's universe that God says can perform some highly specialized operations on your heart.

Because these words are God's words, they are able to teach you in such a way that you can truly and accurately know who God is and what He is like. You can know what God thinks of you and your way of life. You can know what God says is His solution to your struggles. You can know the meaning of life with absolute confidence. You can know how to live a life that delights God rather than enrages Him. You can know how to live a completely contented life without having to depend on pleasant sensory experiences as the central pillar. This is because God's words teach.

Because these words are God's words, they are designed to slip through the most guarded recesses of your heart as a scalpel slips through flesh. God's words are able to reach your most sensitive thoughts, bringing you in an instant to your knees in sorrow for your sin. God's words can strike your inner person in such a way that you will be wounded regardless of how high you hold your homemade shield. God has free access to your naked heart and is able to guide it at will as you are able to guide water with your hand under an open tap (See Proverbs 21:1). Your heart may be as hard as stone. You may be unaffected by anything I can urge on you here, but God's Word will slit you open in the split second He desires to bring you to Himself (See Hebrews 4:12-13). Do you realize God may have already done that in your heart as you have read these few chapters? This is because God's words convict.

Because these words are God's words, they show you where you have gone wrong. They pierce you in order to stop you in your mad rush toward self destruction. Fighting against God is as stupid and futile as fighting against a thorn bush (See Acts 26:14).

But God's Word doesn't leave you eviscerated and moribund. God's words take you in their compassionate hands and nurse you. They restore you to a quality of life you never dreamed possible. They put you back on your feet and hold you there. They set your yearning gaze on the lovely Jesus and move your longing feet in His direction. This is because God's words correct.

Because these words are God's words, they motivate you to apply yourself to Christian disciplines, so that you remain outside of the macabre clutches of your old lusts. These words are always working with a relentless energy (See Hebrews 4:12), driving God's people on to new heights of delighted devotion to Him. God's words are not simply ordinary words, they are alive, and they perform the work God sends them to do (Consider Isaiah 55:10-11, Psalm 33:6, Genesis 1:1). There is something awesome about God's words. This is because God's words train in righteousness.

Armed with these words, a child of God can become complete. God's words can build him up to the point where he is able to meet all challenges. Doesn't that kind of completeness appeal to you, considering the way you have folded every time you are faced with the opportunity to click onto your favorite porn site, throw back your favorite alcoholic beverage, or eat that whole slab of chocolate?

Beyond this completeness, however, God's Word is able to equip you with everything you need to do every good and right thing that you must do from now on to live an exemplary life in God's eyes. In verse seventeen (2 Timothy 3:17), the word that the NIV has translated "thoroughly equipped" is a marine or athletic term. In marine terms, it speaks of a ship standing by the quay, being equipped for a journey into the open ocean. In those days, there was no National Sea Rescue Institute to help you out if you bashed a hole in your hull, so they had to carry spare wood, tar, nails, sails, ropes, etc. In fact, they had to think of everything they would need in any situation they might encounter on the surface of a vast, unpredictable ocean. Their lives depended upon their ability to think of everything they might possibly need.

In athletic terms, an athlete would train frantically for months and years to compete in the games. When he arrived for the contest, he would be able to say he was completely prepared for every demand this event would make on his body. There was nothing he could do to be more thoroughly equipped for this event. He was a finely tuned machine able to perform at optimum levels.

God says the Bible is like that. By absorbing the teachings of Scripture and by disciplining oneself to do what it says, a child of God is thoroughly equipped for any situation that rises up on life's ocean or racetrack. And my argument here is that God has supplied in His Word everything you, as an addict, will need.

Lest you hear me saying that the Bible is a book of techniques by which you can extricate yourself from your problems, I would like to say one more thing about God's words. The Bible is not a book that you can use as you would any other textbook. The Bible embraces great mysteries that will not be found by people who desire to use it to free themselves from misery and discard it. The Bible will not dance to the tune of a selfish agenda to provide the entertainment of personal happiness. The reason this is true is because the Bible is no ordinary book.

As you humble yourself before the Bible, you will find that an air of majesty gusts through its pages. There is the aroma of royalty in its words—a vast glorious essence that will quickly slip away when submerged beneath the mockery of the proud (See James 4:6, 1 Peter 5:5). To the broken heart; to the aching eye; to the yearning, worn-out sinner who is weary with his sin and who comes in repentance, God will draw aside the veil that he may gaze in upon the beauty of the Lord (See Psalm 51:17, Psalm 27:4). Are these living, working words not beyond conception? These words which at the same time can be whispering delightful peace to the soul of the disenchanted simultaneously devour, with gruesome carnage, the arrogant fool.

What is unique to these blessed pages, dear friend, is the Person who lives in them. As you weep in sorrow over these pages, reading God's account of redemptive history, the essence of which is beyond description, you become aware that you are not alone. You once looked upon the black marks on a white Bible page and said, "I've tried Jesus, but He hasn't helped me. I've heard all of this stuff before." You are now gazing not at mere words on paper but into the shocking beauty of the face of Christ. His loveliness surpasses description—as does His grace in showing Himself to those who have persisted in such violence against Him (See Romans 8:7). Beware of the temptation to flick through the pages of Holy Scripture, viewing them as the mere scribbles of any religious author. Rather, the Bible is the treasure chest in which the delightful, almighty God is discovered.

Nothing compares to the sudden blast of infinite power, as you urgently search for Christ in the words of Scripture, when God thrusts His arms deep into your inner person, laying hold of your old, cynical heart of stone, and, slinging it into oblivion, implants within you a wonderful, new, soft heart of flesh (See Ezekiel 36:26, Deuteronomy 30:6, John 3:3, 2 Corinthians 5:17).

This is what happened to my grandfather who was a drunkard until he was thirty-two years old. He was facing a divorce and poverty as a result of his lifestyle. One evening he went to fetch his kids from a Sunday school presentation of John Bunyan's *Pilgrim's Progress*. He arrived a little early and sat in the back row, waiting for the lesson to end.

In a moment, the Word of God spoke deep into his heart, slicing him open, driving him to see his spiritual poverty before God. God saved him that night as he confessed his lifelong rebellion against God and his indulgence in pleasant sensory experiences. The Lord changed him so radically and made him such a student of the Word that he was preaching the gospel within two years. The Lord saved many other people through his life, and he died a dearly loved child of God. Praise the Lord for this remarkable work in an alcoholic's life.

My dear brother Wayne was enslaved to drugs for twelve years. The Lord arrested him by His grace, and he lived as an outstanding trophy of that grace until the Lord called him home to glory in 2004. There are millions of life stories like this in heaven and on earth. Jesus really does save.

So what kind of response am I hoping to draw from you at this point? I'm asking you to hear, as we have just concluded, that God does have a solution to your particular struggle. This is not just another rabbit path to follow that will simply lead you to another dark hole. Take hope! Consider the degree of your struggles and know that the power of God to rescue you from your misery for His glory is incalculably greater. If you have truly grasped the greatness of God's salvation, even now you will feel a great new hope welling up within you. Lay down your weapons and come out to your Maker with your hands up (See Acts 17:30). Cease your struggle against Him. Without this, you have no solution, no hope, no God. God's salvation is the only effective cure known to man for the craving heart.

Chapter 4

DELIBERATE FREEFALL

I N THE EARLY nineties, I stood deep in thought on a pavement in Hillbrow in the city of Johannesburg. I was looking at a man lying face-down on the pavement. In the major cities of the world, this is, of course, a familiar sight. The difference with this man was that this was where he had suddenly stopped after a twenty-two storey plummet. There he lay. A grizzly discovery.

Stunned bystanders who had called the ambulance chipped in fragments of information, creating a sketch of the events surrounding this man's demise. He and some friends had been playing around at the pool, twenty-two floors up on the top of a block of flats when, quite inexplicably, he had dropped over the precipice. It had been an accident. He hadn't intended to destroy himself but had still been listening to music on his portable player, fragments of which littered the sidewalk and street. Long strands of fine cassette tape dancing in the breeze.

"It happened so quickly," they exclaimed, as I was concluding the same. So quickly, yet the fall seemed to him an eternity.

Moments flashed by like days, crammed with dread terror as the ground rushed up, hard and merciless to smash him. There was nothing he could do as his terrified scream mingled with the roar in his ears and was punctuated by a thud. Oh, the violent dismay of those remaining moments. So unnecessary. So sudden. So final.

If you have struggled in your addiction for any length of time, you have tasted this sense of horror in your private sins—you have suddenly been gripped by the fear that you just can't stop. You are rushing to your own destruction. Your future is harsh and cruel. The ground is blasting toward your tender flesh to crush and mortify. You started out like this wretched man, playing around on the roof—a little fun, a little experimentation, a little flirting. You began as the master, and your porn was your slave giving you the pleasant sensory experience you loved. It was a nice little secret you held from your wife, your family, your church. The man on the roof was in control until quite suddenly, he wasn't. Have you tipped over the edge? Is your neat little sin now controlling you? Has the master become the slave? Is your habit demanding that you spend more and more time, money, devotion, energy on it? Have you fallen in love with your sin so desperately that you are now its slave?

Jesus said to some people who thought they were safe, "I tell you the truth, everyone who sins is a slave to sin." (John 8:34). The grammar dictates that the person who is in a continuous habit or practice of sin is trapped in that sin in the same way that this man was trapped in his fall. In the act of pursuing your pleasant sensory experiences, you are actively jumping to your own destruction. No amount of good resolve will free you from this gravitational pull. Many addicts have told me aggressively that they can stop. They don't need help. If you have that same attitude, you are putting your word up against the Word of God. This is a fearful thing.

Some other things that won't help a falling man are warnings that he is destroying his body. You've heard all of these stories before. This stuff destroys your heart. This stuff destroys your lungs. This stuff destroys your brain, etc. Yeah, yeah. Warnings about how you are wrecking your body no longer spike your interest. You know you are wrecking your body, but you still have enough health to hobble over to the bottle store and throw a few more shots down the hatch. It is still your favorite pleasant sensory experience.

What you, as a slave to your favorite sin, have surely discovered, in addition, is that a slave can't rest. How it distresses me to see in addicts the compulsion to move. An addict in a rehab center is happy to be off the streets, to have a comfortable bed to sleep in, and a belly full of good food. But within days the itch begins. He has no plans, no place to go, no reason to leave, yet there is a deep restlessness within that commands him to go—to move. He can't sit still. The compulsion becomes a frantic demand, "I can't stay here. I have to move." This is like Cain in Genesis 4:12 and 14. He became a restless wanderer. He couldn't settle down. Wherever he was, he had to be somewhere else. Aren't you weary of this slavery?

As you plummet down the vertical surface of this building in your final seconds, feeling the terror of destruction, you fly past the windows on each floor. Every window represents a lost opportunity. While you are falling to your death in your pursuit of heroin or coke, you are losing opportunities that you will never have again. You can't concentrate at school or work, so you are losing the opportunity to excel in your studies or work. Those days will never return. You are noticing that your health is suffering. You get no exercise, no proper food, and no proper sleep. You are wasting away. You are flying past these windows of opportunity forever. The life you dreamt of when you were a child is melting like ice-cream in the sun of your frantic habit.

You plummet past the opportunity to enjoy a happy, married life. Your communication and close relationship is replaced by deception and avoidance. Sex is no longer a beautiful demonstration of love—but a battleground. Your first love is gone. You can't stand all of the pleading of your wife and kids who are in obvious pain. Rather than dealing honestly with your relationships with your wife and kids, you recede to the comforts of a pleasant sensory experience: your internet chat group, your bottle, or your syringe. This is a wasted life filled with opportunities you will never have back.

Other windows are the opportunities to use your time and money well so you don't have to live with galling regret. These too are gone forever. Your money is only worth what it will buy you in pleasant sensory experience. Having lost the opportunity to make and keep good friends, you become universally unpopular, skulking around with other people who are also unwelcome.

You claim to have a relationship with God, but you have no power to pray, read the Bible, study, witness, be involved in the church. Your Christianity is in words only. When confronted, you are consumed by strong emotions, anger, sorrow, guilt, and bitterness that you can't put your finger on, but it is massively unpleasant.

The reason I have insisted on laboring this point is because as an addict you are fully aware of all of these miseries you face, and yet, not even all of these miseries and lost opportunities are enough to drive you to lay down this damning habit that has you in a stranglehold. Is it not obvious that you are a slave? Is it not obvious that you are trapped? Is it not obvious that you are falling to your own destruction in your dastardly pursuit of pleasant sensory experiences? You are a victim.

Dear friend, I really do see you as trapped and completely unable to pull yourself out of your free fall. You really cannot escape. And I say to my dear Christian brothers and sisters who desire to help addicts. This you must understand. He really is trapped. He really is falling to his death. He really will be crushed under the gruesome consequences of his sin. This should fill you with pity. The thought of this helpless plummet and the inevitable destruction should move you to reach out to this wasted man or woman with the patience and compassion of the Lord Jesus Christ. He truly is a victim. He is subject to the temporal and eternal desolation that awaits such a person.

After observing this cruel slavery, some sectors have dogmatically asserted that the addict has a disease. In the same way that one person falls to the destructive effects of cancer, so also addicts have fallen prey to a disease to which they are victim. Please don't hear me saying that. If you, in your slavery to your personal sin, imbibe the lie that you are the helpless victim of a foul disease, then, you can have no hope at all. To be the hopeless victim of a disease without a cure is to have no hope of recovery. I don't want to rob you of hope. On the contrary, I believe there is more hope for you than you have ever imagined.

"You are contradicting yourself," you object. "You just said that I am a victim, then you said I'm not a victim." Good, you've been reading well. Yes, as an addict you are a victim, but that's not the end of the story. While the disease mentality continues to permeate western society, the Bible has a far more mature and hopeful interpretation of your struggles. Please follow me as we unfold another life-giving truth from Scripture.

Allow me to begin with another illustration. In 2001 Christine McCafferty and Peter Hammond wrote in their book, *The Pink Agenda*,

> In 1999 it emerged that the latest trend among some in the "gay community" in San Francisco is for HIV-negative men to have unprotected sodomy with HIV-positive men *for the "thrill of contact with the deadly AIDS virus."*

The author goes on to say that 18,000 homosexual men have already died of AIDS in San Francisco since 1981 when AIDS was discovered there.[10]

In this quote that reveals something of the heart of slavery to homosexual sin, we see an element that goes beyond mere slavery, beyond mere "victimhood." It is an element that caulks immeasurable hope into the equation. I say this because in the quote and in the lifestyles of addicts, I see a volitional element involved in their pursuits. This willing participation goes beyond the description of mere helpless slavery.

Consider a further illustration used by Jerry Wragg at the South African Shepherd's Conference a few years ago that will clarify the point I am making.

It is said that while Eskimos have always utilised polar bears for their fur, bones, and meat, they have a problem. Eskimos are small and polar bears are big with long, powerful forelimbs that could decapitate an Eskimo with one swipe. Because bears are poor negotiators, Eskimos had to develop a system that would keep them safe and at the same time avail them of the polar bear's useful features. Having bored a hole in the ice, they would insert the long handle of a specially designed knife so that the handle would freeze into the ice leaving the blade projecting vertically into the air. They would then slaughter a smaller animal and drag it in large circuits around the knife and eventually impale the carcass on the knife.

Because polar bears can smell blood at a distance of approximately sixteen miles, it is not long before one comes to investigate. The bear begins to lick up the blood on the ice, coming closer and closer to the carcass. Eventually, the ice is clean, and he begins to eat the carcass from the knife. Having eaten the flesh, he continues to lick the blood off the knife. The bear is not content until he has licked up all of the blood, so he licks and licks the knife, slicing his tongue, causing profuse bleeding. The more he licks the more blood there is. Before long this bewitching ritual takes its toll on the mighty bear who collapses onto the ice, weak from blood loss. The Eskimos then rush out from their concealed positions and club the fallen bear to death.

Yes, the bear is a victim. But at the same time, he continues to subject himself to the actions that bring him crashing down. As an addict, you will confess, you are exactly the same as that bear as you play "spot the rock" on the carpet. You are a victim of your own deliberate pursuit of pleasant sensory experiences. You are simultaneously a victim and a violator. There is a volitional element to your addiction.

You are like the man falling from the building who comes to a wretched end, but in your case you are coming to a wretched end because you have deliberately jumped and continue to jump and jump and jump. This is what God is saying in Romans 3:23. You have sinned in the past and there is nothing you can do to go back and erase those sins. All have sinned. You are trapped with that bad record. What is more horrible than that is that you go on and on falling short of God's standard by inclination. You are trapped in a lifestyle that enrages God because you willingly choose pleasant sensory experiences, pushing down God's demands (See Romans 1:18).

You will know what I am speaking about when I say that you will refuse to stop licking. You will refuse to stop spiking heroin. You will refuse to stop looking at nakedness. You will refuse to stop driving too fast. You will refuse to stop guzzling beer. You will refuse to stop engorging yourself on chocolate. You will refuse to stop "letting rip" in your anger. You will refuse to control your urge to sleep more than you need to. You will refuse to stop licking. And as the bear sinks into ruin, licking the knife, you slump into misery indulging in just another small concession to your flesh. Little by little there is less and less room for God in your chain of pleasant sensory experiences even where those pleasant sensory experiences are not sinful in themselves. Thomas Watson says, "A sinner will rather lose Christ and heaven than his lusts."

The reason I have labored this point is that Scripture labors this point. While Scripture sees addicts as victims, it also sees them as violators. Permit me to show you a few examples. Ephesians 2:3 uses the following language, "All of us also lived among them at one time, *gratifying the cravings* of our sinful nature and *following* its desires and thoughts. Like the rest, we were by nature objects of wrath."[11] Here, every unsaved person is falling victim to the wrath of God, because he continually pursues his lusts. The wrath he incurs is seen both in the immediate consequences of his lifestyle in this world, and then in the eternal consequences he will reap as he passes into eternity without Christ.

Then in 4:19, Paul continues,

> Having lost all sensitivity, they have *given themselves over* to sensuality so as to *indulge* in every kind of impurity, with a continual lust for more.[12]

It is impossible to deny the deliberate, volitional element the Bible attributes to sinners who habitually engage in personal sin.

Before concluding this point, there is one more text I would like to mention. Peter says, "For you have spent enough time in the past doing what pagans *choose* to do—living in debauchery, lust, drunkenness, orgies, carousing and detestable idolatry." (1 Peter 4:3).[13] Here again is the intentional choosing to engage in all kinds of sinful pursuits.

The question should still be in your mind, "So how can the fact that an addict chooses to destroy himself give him hope?" As an addict suffering under the consequences of your volitional slavery, you have hope because it is your misery that pushes you to the point of desperation before God. Your sufferings and your wretchedness are designed to make you desperate. As the falling man bellows in hellish agony, dropping to the concrete, so your sufferings are engineered to open your eyes to your need, your frailty, your vulnerability. You are an object of God's fiery wrath and you are plummeting to your death as a consequence of your own sin.

You will agree with me that without this mercy, without this compelling gracious act of God, pushing you to the point of frantic despair, you would never stop. You would never cry out for mercy because you are too much in love with your sin. You love it too much to stop. God is pushing you to scream out, "Lord help! God have mercy on me a sinner." God is driving you to this extreme because you are guilty of your sin.

Do you see now how it is that you have hope if you deliberately choose to sin? Because God forgives sin. God doesn't forgive disease, the very thought is absurd. Who ever confessed to God the sin of contracting the flu virus or malaria? No, God both forgives sin and saves from sin. God says, "If you confess your sins to God, [saying about your own lusting heart what God says about it] He is faithful and just to forgive you your sins and to purify you from all unrighteousness." (1 John 1:9). God is able to save you completely if you come to Him through Christ (See Hebrews 7:25). He is able to perform a rescue mission in your life that will radically free you from the power of your sin and its consequences.

Before you come to Jesus for salvation, you are facing every ounce of the consequences that you have stored up for yourself (See Romans 2:5). As the wind roars in your ears and you see ferocious calamity unlock its jaws to receive your tender frame, you begin to scream out to God for mercy. You can't stop. You have deliberately jumped into this guilty plunge. But now you are begging God for undeserved favor. In an instant the great Savior, fired with infinite passion, strides forward in all His effulgent glory. He is clothed in a robe stained with blood and on His head is a crown of your sins. Never more the immeasurable thrill of His Father's heart, He reaches out for you in your helpless plunge, nestling you in His soft hands of mercy, breaking your fall. And the great Savior continues to fall in your place.

With shocked amazement, from your new place of eternal safety in the hand of God, you stare at the unspeakable carnage into which your Savior plunges instead of you. The fiery anger of God that should have been directed at you in that instant explodes in the face of Jesus. Before your eyes he, as it were, impacts that sidewalk, bearing the brunt of your consequences, and bursts open, splattering across the street. There you see the dreadful result of your sin to your Savior, whose suffering in reality was indescribably more extreme and macabre. See His lovely form hanging on the cross, smashed, bruised, lacerated, and crushed as your substitute (See 1 Peter 3:18).

I beg you to hear this warning—you can't stop! You need to be rescued, saved. Don't be like the people described in Revelation 16:10-11 who suffered to the point of gnawing their own tongues in agony because of their sinful lifestyles and rejection of God, yet, they continue to curse God and refuse to repent. God is driving you to your knees in repentance through your sufferings as an addict. God desires you to confess your sins to Him, and He will forgive you (1 John 1:9).

See how the Lord did this to all kinds of people involved in all kinds of different sinful lifestyles in Psalm 107. This Psalm is a psalm of praise and gratitude for the goodness of God. His goodness is seen in subjecting wilful sinners to hardships in order to bring them to Himself in desperation, in repentance. In verses ten and eleven you may see yourself trapped in the misery of your sin. In verse twelve, take note of the words, "so he subjected them to bitter labor…" What was the result? Verse thirteen says, "Then they cried to the LORD in their trouble, and he saved them from their distress." Call out, like Peter did in Matthew 14:30, "Lord, save me!" "And everyone who calls on the name of the Lord will be saved." (Acts 2:21, Romans 10:13)

Chapter 5

BUT GOD HASN'T
HELPED ME

A LITTLE-KNOWN HERO, native to South Africa, was featured in a small article in a local newspaper. He was walking along the sidewalk on his way to work when he noticed smoke belching from the windows of his boss's house. He was obviously the first person on the scene and immediately determined to do what he could.

It was obvious to our hero that something was happening in that house and that something was very likely to be fire. Even though he didn't know the details—how it started, in what room it was, who was inside the house, etc., he had a very good idea that his boss's house was on fire.

Let me now seize an issue that many addicts struggle with when they are confronted, in their agony, with the gospel. Maybe this chapter will express exactly what you have been thinking but have been afraid to admit. You have broken down in tears, insisting that you have repented and have confessed your sins and have tried to change, but the Christian life is devoid of power for you. You believe that in spite of your pleading with God, He hasn't helped you. Please pay close attention to this chapter because it is absolutely crucial in your fight.

Let me begin by saying that the addicted life is very much like that burning house. While people who live around you are not sure of the exact details of your addiction, they do see the smoke belching from the windows of your life. You can't hide your addiction for long, in most cases, because people begin to suspect that something is going on in your life. Just as our hero suspected fire, the people around you suspect addiction.

You may ask, "What are you talking about?" Consider the following examples of "smoke" that people see emitting from an addict's life.[14]

If you are a husband, your wife may notice that there seems to be less money in the home in spite of the fact that your job hasn't changed. You become touchy when she mentions it. This is "smoke."

If you are a wife, your husband notices that you seem to be getting unusually irritable or exhausted. You sigh in despair. The house is a mess, and you are defensive. This is "smoke."

If you are a son who has always been close to your family, your parents may notice you have started spending a lot of time alone in your room with the door closed. When you come out, instead of spending time with them, you avoid them. It is clear to them that you have changed your group of friends and you have become strangely secretive. This is "smoke."

If you are a daughter, your parents may have noticed you developing an unusual resistance to wise advice. They may have even caught you lying to cover something up. They just can't put their finger on it, but from what they see, your attitude has changed and you are not the way you used to be. This is "smoke."

You may have begun to lose weight dramatically—others have noticed. You may have been experiencing constant colds or sinus problems—other people can see it.

Have you become unusually tired or restless at times? Are your eyes sometimes red, your eyelids droopy, or your pupils unusually large or small? Are you experiencing extraordinary depression, moodiness or a suicidal tendency? Have you begun to experience changes in your personality? These are "smoke."

Have other people noticed the smells of alcohol or smoke on you? Have other people found your drugs, syringes, spoons, straws, or other telling items among your personal things? These are "smoke."

It is not uncommon for other people to notice things about you that you don't realize you have exposed. Others, especially those who have had experience in this area, can see the smoke escaping from the cracks of your carefully concealed secret. Paul says in Galatians 5:19 that the acts of the sinful nature are obvious. The Greek word he uses there is *phaneros* which is the adjective of the word *phainō* which means to shine. It speaks of something that is plain, hence the NIV word obvious.[15] When you indulge yourself in sinful habits, your actions have that quality about them that makes them *shine*. You can't keep a sinful life a secret, someone finds out sooner or later. It is obvious from the "smoke" in your life that you are tangled up in the sinful pursuit of some pleasant sensory experience.

I mention this "smoke" because this is what is going to attract people—like the hero in our story—who desire to help you. Your addiction is obvious to them, and if you know people who genuinely care about you, don't be surprised if they come bursting into your life to rescue you. They can see the smoke trail drawn from your stricken plane as it streaks toward earth. While you may perceive their helpfulness as intrusion, it really is genuine concern.

Not only is the smoke of your addiction obvious to other people, it is obvious to you as well. Your life and options are becoming narrower and more restricted week by week, day by day, less noticeable at first, but then alarmingly quickly.

After running to the front door of the house, finding it unlocked, our hero burst in to rescue his boss. Seeing no-one, he made his way to a closed bedroom door and thrust it aside. The inferno inside breathed its scorching welcome into his heaving lungs while the smoke laid its hazy hand over his eyes. After recomposing himself, he made out through the blaze beyond another open door, the figure of a man in a bathroom clinging to the steel bars that covered a small window. Charging in, our hero found his boss in the throes of despair, ready to collapse, his skin blistered from the heat, but still alive. There was still hope.

Like that man, you are finding your options painfully narrowed to the point where even the thought of running to safety is beyond conception. He, like you, lost control through an ordinary sequence of events. It turned out that the boss in question had been a heavy smoker. That morning, it seems, he had woken up and lit up. As he dozed in his bed with a cigarette, he had fallen asleep, dropping his little firebrand onto the welcoming blankets. Waking up to the smell of smoke, he had alighted from his bed and gone—still unhurried—to the bathroom to get some water to douse the fire now kindled in his room. Yes, it was a fire, but certainly not out of his control. Unfortunately, he hadn't managed to secure a suitable container in which to carry the water and upon turning back to his bedroom, found it impassable. He had trapped himself in what had become a life-and-death situation by an ordinary sequence of events.

You also have found yourself trapped by an ordinary sequence of events. I don't know what your particular thing is, but it may have begun with that first cigarette, that first joint, or simply flicking through the pages of a porn magazine. You can still look back to the ordinary way in which you stepped closer and closer to the edge, and you are now in free-fall. You are now trapped in agony, wishing you had resisted the urge in the first place. None of this damage would have been done. Rather, you find yourself descending into misery with the flames beginning to lick off the outer layers of your skin.

You have been busted and exposed, something you would pray-to-God would never happen. Now everyone sees you in a different way, and they treat you differently. You always seem to be letting them down, and they don't take you seriously anymore. You get no respect, and you feel you have earned none. Friend by friend and family member by family member, you have made yourself unwelcome by lying, deceiving, manipulating, and stealing. You have lost yet another job and can't find another—a problem that is compounded by the fact that you have lost your desire to even earn a living. With your joblessness comes "cashlessness." You have to beg for money wherever you go and as a result, everyone who sees you coming avoids you. You are forced to walk everywhere you go unless you can bum a ride from someone. You have worn out even your closest friends and supporters. All this time, you nurse your injured pride and look bitterly at how unfairly you have been treated.

Eventually, you are like a stray dog wandering the streets, digging through rubbish bins for scraps. The world has become a hard place. The heat is unbearable. Your skin begins to blister as you dangle from the bars of your squashed enclosure—moments before the searing draught chars your airways and you slump to the floorboards. You are impoverished. You cry out, wailing in the dark alleyways to the deaf concrete ears of the city. You are an exhausted addict. No-one wants you, seemingly, not even God. By pursuing your pleasant sensory experiences, all of the things that bring you the most satisfaction—all you have managed to secure—is a squatter camp, a slum, squalor. You have been pursuing paradise where all of your cherished dreams gather around you into a soft nest, yet your dream has vanished and you have plopped into the sewer of life.

It is in this misery that you become aware of the struggle that is the concern of this chapter. It is at this point of exhaustion—at this point where you have no-one to call and no resources upon which to rely, that you begin to focus upon God. You begin to call out to Him, but discover that nothing happens. You protest that you have prayed and prayed to God, but He hasn't helped you. You can't imagine a hell that is worse than the onslaught raised against you now. But doesn't the Bible say that everyone who calls on the name of the Lord will be saved? (Joel 2:32, Acts 2:21, Romans 10:13). You are shouting out because you are cornered and burning and in pain.

I assure you, God knows about your pain and the ignominy of your plight. So much so that He has been careful to describe it well in Scripture. Please read very carefully at this point.

I have named this situation I have labored to describe, the *"metamélomai phenomenon."* The reason I have given it such a name is because the word *metamélomai* is a Greek word used in the New Testament to describe exactly this predicament. To experience this metamélomai phenomenon is to experience an absolutely devastating thing. Allow me to expand on this by showing how two people in the Bible experienced it.

The first is a man who had one of the greatest inheritances ever at his fingertips. Unfortunately, he chose the immediate enjoyment of a pleasant sensory experience over the rich inheritance that was his. One day he came in from hunting, and he was hungry. In order to satisfy his hunger, he sold his inheritance for a bowl of soup. Read the text with me.

> See to it that no one is sexually immoral, or is godless like Esau, who for a single meal sold his inheritance rights as the oldest son. Afterwards, as you know, when he wanted to inherit this blessing, he was rejected. He could bring about no change of mind, though he sought the blessing with tears."
> —Hebrews 12:16-17

Do you see what God says about this man? He was willing to blindly throw away all future blessing for that immediate pleasant sensory experience. God calls this godlessness. The time arrived for him when the bowl of soup had already been digested and forgotten for many years, and he longed for something more. He wanted the blessings he had sold, but they were out of his reach. They belonged to someone else.

He fell into a sorrow like the sorrow you are experiencing in the metamélomai phenomenon. He sought the blessing with tears. The Greek word for "sought" is synonymous with begging and craving.[16] Just as you have longed and begged for God to rescue you from this mess, Esau, a robust man, cried like a baby for the blessings he craved.

What makes this text so unique is that it also uses another pivotal word in this transaction. Although Esau cried and begged and craved the blessings, the good things he had lost and would never enjoy, he never came to the point of *metánoia*. That is, he never came to the point of true repentance (translated "change of mind" in the NIV). *Metánoia* is the word the New Testament and the Septuagint (the Greek translation of the Old Testament) use for true repentance.

Is it not astounding to you that a person could be in tears, in sorrow, grovelling on the ground, praying to God, calling out in agony, and yet not repenting? "What is the difference?" you may ask. The difference is that the person who is absorbed in the throes of the metamélomai phenomenon is experiencing extreme regret and negative emotions over the things he has lost and will possibly never have again. He is consumed with the negative sensory experiences he is enduring and is mourning the fact that he is unable to raise himself up to the satisfaction of pleasant sensory experiences again. It is as if he has a wallet stuffed with cash, and he drops it over a bridge into a river from which it can never be recovered. The person experiencing the metamélomai phenomenon is bewailing his loss. Don't fail to notice that the metamélomai phenomenon goes no further than negative emotions over what has been lost. By definition it is regret over personal loss.[17]

The metamélomai phenomenon is in contrast with true repentance (*metánoia*) in that it doesn't grieve over wrongness of your actions before God but primarily over personal loss.

Let's step closer to the groans of the other man in the Bible who experienced this metamélomai phenomenon. He was in a truly privileged position. He lived in the age when God Himself became a man and lived by his side. After fellowship with the Christ, eating His food, drinking His drink, this man was confronted with something that caused his senses to tingle.

Judas knew that Christ had outstanding miraculous powers. Judas knew that Christ would become a great ruler. Judas knew that he stood in line to share in great honor as one of Christ's closest companions when Christ came into His glory. But in spite of all he knew there was something else that had arrested Judas' attention—the little pouch that contained the money. The thrill, the pleasant sensory experience of dipping into the cash, was so delightful to him that he would gladly sacrifice his fellowship with Christ for it. All that mattered to him was the immediate gratification of having money and using it secretly for his own selfish ends. Judas was a thief. (John 12:6).

This trend in his life continued up to the point where he had to face the final ultimatum: would he choose the handful of coins or God incarnate? What were overwhelmingly colorful to him were the jingling coins and the satisfaction they could buy him. They screamed a false value from their little bag. Reaching out his hand, he condemned his close friend (See Psalm 55:12-13). All he had to do was betray Jesus and the money was all his.

Oh, the magnitude of the sin he was committing was beyond the capacity of his blind eyes. After Judas had betrayed Jesus and saw Him condemned, Matthew 27:3 says he was, "seized with remorse." What was it that was galling him? You may conclude that he realized that he had done wrong by the fact that in verse four he declared, "I have sinned." But what was he feeling? He was seized with *metamélomai*. He was filled with regret over what he had done. He wished he hadn't done it. He wished he could take back that action. He was so gripped by that *metamélomai* that he went away and hanged himself (verse five).

There are two things here that are shocking. The first is that the fallen human heart is so sinful that we will choose pleasant sensory experiences over the Lord of glory. The second is that even while we are experiencing regret, even to the point of suicide, we can even come to the point of acknowledging that what we have done is sin, and still not drive further and come to true repentance. If Judas had been truly repentant, he would have been forgiven even for that sin. His suicide was a demonstration that he was not willing to face Christ and the disciples, confess his sin, receive God's forgiveness, and begin to work on a new life. There is a vast difference between regret and repentance.

Another case that should still be fresh in your mind is that of Candi, who was exposed to her parents by her ex-boyfriend after being involved in making pornographic DVDs and selling them over the internet. Consider her words. While in rehab for depression, she told of her deep shame and remorse for what she did to herself. "I hate myself. How could I get involved with this smut? I thought I was so cool, and now I just feel like a dirty, slutty girl. My life feels as if it is over. I hate what I have done to my parents, the disappointment and hurt."[18] Do you hear the voice of the metamélomai phenomenon?

So what hope do you have as you burn to death in your claustrophobic dungeon? Can you really change? Can your life ever be turned around?

Because of the importance of the answer to this question, I would like to devote the whole next chapter to it.

Chapter 6

LIFESAVING
CONVICTION

BEFORE I EVEN begin with God's answer to the devastating metamélomai phenomenon introduced in the previous chapter, let me briefly deal with one principle. In your agony and the fervency with which you have begged God for mercy, you will be tempted to think that you are doing everything you can possibly do, but that God is not doing what He should be doing in response. Because the sinful mind is hostile toward God (See Romans 8:7), this kind of thinking comes naturally.

Please beware of entertaining such a thought, which is far from the truth. Deuteronomy 32:3 declares that God is always consistent, perfect, just, faithful, and right. If you are convinced that God has done wrong in your case, I urge you to withdraw that conclusion. It is a fearful thing to insist that you are calling on the name of the Lord, but He is not saving you. Settle it as a final principle in your mind, even as you read this page, that regardless of how the situation may seem, if you see God as the Person in the wrong, you have come to the wrong conclusion.

God can never be at fault. Having established that, shall we see how to move forward from the metamélomai phenomenon?

Many people, Christians included, believe that an addict must first hit "rock bottom" before he can truly change. Do you believe that? As I ask that question I see you in my mind's eye, nodding wisely, having imbibed some pop psychology over the coffee table. If a Christian person desires to see you, an addict, radically saved, does he need to wait for you to hit rock bottom before you can turn around? Let me ask you this question in a different way. Must a Christian who cares for you stand at the door of the burning house and watch you burn to death, or should he attempt to rescue you while there is still time? The hero in our story didn't sit around. He rushed into that burning building with a sense of desperation. A life was at stake. He felt compelled to do everything within his power to help.

In this true story, our hero, after finding his boss in that grim state in his bathroom, shouting through the open window for help, performed a rescue. He dragged his exhausted boss through the bedroom where the fire blazed, through the lounge, and into the cool safety of the garden. If he had waited any longer, the rescue would have been impossible. Time was critical. Time is still critical.

So here stands a Christian friend. He can see you frying in the bathroom, and he knows he needs to perform a rescue. What is he going to do? What tools does he have at his disposal? As a believer, he has rescue tools that the world knows nothing of. He is responsible before God to use them well. Let's go over his inventory.

He has the Savior. He knows the Lord who saved him. He knows the ignorance he walked in before the Lord saved him.

He knows the way in which he fell in love with Christ and how God gave him a desire to live a clean life to please Him. He knows the passion in God's heart for him and for other sinners who are still lost—burning in the misery of their sin. He sees that passion demonstrated not only on the cross at Golgotha, but in Christ's perfect life of obedience, lived on his behalf. His (your rescuer's) life-record was totally messed up, but Jesus lived an exemplary life that has completely delighted God's heart. He understands by faith that Jesus has given him His royal clothes of righteousness to wear in front of God so that God is as pleased with him as He is with Jesus.

He knows this Jesus and has a deep, everlasting relationship with Him. He knows that if Christ saved him in the way He did, transforming his life, he can have every confidence that Christ can do the same for any other sinner, no matter how ruined his life may be. Your rescuer kits up to come to your rescue knowing that it is not ultimately him who will save you, but God. It is the Savior who will save you through this Christian rescuer's actions. He is able to save any sinner (See Hebrews 7:25, James 4:12).

Your Christian rescuer also has the Holy Spirit. It is He whom Christ has given to live inside of His people. He motivates them toward personal holiness. He helps them to understand God's Word when they read it. One of the things you, as an addict, have probably discovered is that when you face the prospect of beginning a new life, what you struggle with most is the sheer motivation to actually do it. To slump back into the pursuit of pleasant sensory experiences is so much easier—it brings immediate physical relief from any struggles.

As your Christian rescuer faces you, he knows that he can depend on the Holy Spirit to power you into the Christian life and see you through to the end. He knows that it is God the Holy Spirit who gives any motivation at all to live the Christian life. All the desire this Christian has for God is from Him. Your Christian rescuer will arm himself with the knowledge that if God saves you, He will complete the work He has begun (See Philippians 1:6).

Third, he has Scripture. I have deliberately not focused on the first two resources because my aim is to focus a little more on this resource, Scripture. Remember that while the world scoffs at Christians' allegiance to the Bible, Christians know that it is through using the words of God that God is most pleased to bring about radical changes in sinners' lives. Using the Bible appears so primitive and insignificant, yet what seems to be the case is very misleading.

Specifically, your rescuer knows two things about the Bible, and he will use this knowledge in his rescue mission to you as you are trapped in the misery of your addiction.

The first thing he knows is found in 2 Timothy 3:15. There, Paul teaches Timothy that it is Scripture which is able to make a person wise for salvation through faith in Jesus Christ. The Bible is the tool God uses in the salvation of sinners. To you, as an addict, this means that God saves miserable addicts through exposure to His Word, the Bible. As your rescuer approaches you, nervous at the greatness of the mission, he is armed with the confidence that he has the resource that God is most likely to use to change your life forever. He has the most professional and efficient equipment a rescuer can have for a rescue such as this.

The second thing he knows is the truth of the next two verses, 2 Timothy 3:16-17. God's Word is the means through which God teaches, convicts, corrects, and trains His people in righteousness. This exposure to and specialized use of the Bible is what builds a believer up to the point where he is considered complete and thoroughly equipped for every good work. Applied to you, this means that God saves and builds miserable addicts up through exposure to His sufficient Word. In order to perform a proper rescue, your Christian rescuer has become proficient in using God's Word in the way God says he should in 2 Timothy 3:15-17. If you would like to know more about this, please read Dr. Jay E. Adams's *How to Help People Change.*[19]

Even more specifically, I would like to focus on one word in that group of words in 2 Timothy 3:16. It is translated *rebuking* or *reproof* in most of the English translations. The word is translated as *convicting* in three English versions and also in Dr. Jay E. Adams's *Christian Counselor's New Testament.*[20]

The reason I mention this is because I am convinced that God speaks most powerfully through Christian rescuers when they give proper attention to 'convicting' addicts of sin through the word. Remember we already showed the inconceivable hope in the fact that addictions are a form of deliberate sin. The reason there is hope is because God forgives sin and not disease. This consideration takes that conclusion to the next step. Your Christian rescuer will convict you of your sin by using the Bible. I would like to explain a little more in order to color in this picture.

This life-saving technique is the act of confronting you. But he will confront you in such a way that you will be convicted of sin. (Even as I write this, I can see in my mind's eye the psychologized reader rolling his eyeballs at such an antiquated idea.) When I say confront and convict, I am not saying that he will storm up to you, rip you out of your casual slouching demeanour by the front of your t-shirt, and bellow into your face. I am speaking of confrontation in love. I am speaking about a rescuer who is driven by such a concern for your soul that he will approach you with a deep sense of sorrow at your wasted life (See Ephesians 4:15). God is not receiving the glory that your life owes Him. Your rescuer fears that God will judge you and desires to see you rescued from that terrible prospect.

To describe the kind of conviction you can expect to be of most benefit to you spiritually, I will compare it to the kind of conviction you would find in a courtroom. Suppose you have broken the law by driving drunk. You are arrested, tested, and incarcerated. On the day of your trial, the magistrate hears the evidence against you, and there is no doubt that you did in fact break the law. In a clear-cut case, the magistrate finds you guilty.

Suppose you then think about it and realize that if this judgement sticks, you will be fined heavily, have your driver's licence revoked, and you won't be able to be re-tested for five years. You decide that you will appeal. You shout out, "But, Your Honor, I don't feel guilty, so I can't be guilty." The question is this: will the fact that you don't feel guilty change the fact that you have broken the law by your actions? Of course not. You are guilty whether you feel it or not.

In this sense of conviction, your Christian rescuer is called upon to build such a case against you that you are proved guilty of sin before God. It makes no difference whether you immediately accept this verdict and repent or whether you laugh it off, the fact is, you are guilty objectively before God. This is an absolutely crucial step in his efforts to help you. Be prepared to receive this confrontation as a gesture of love.

In order to convict, it is essential that the Christian rescuer bring his arguments out of the general, abstract arena and into specific facts about the here and now of your sin. In order for you, or any sinner, to confess his sin to God and to receive God's forgiveness, it is helpful for you to be convicted of specific sins. I have prepared a suggestion on how you can expect a Christian to convict you of sin with specific facts, based on an actual case.

My son, I love you. For years you have brought amazing joy to my heart. But today I have to speak to you in love because I can see you are in danger. Your life has been changing, and the latest changes I have seen bring tears to my eyes and pain to my heart. The final thing that has moved me to speak to you was what happened on Tuesday evening. After running away from the rehabilitation center, you went sneaking around my house, the home of your very own father, and levered the aluminium window frame open with this screwdriver. You broke in and stole my DVD machine and your sister's computer.

My son, do you realize that my grief is not your only concern? God says in 1 Corinthians 6:10 that drunkards and thieves will not inherit the Kingdom of God. Do you realize that you are that drunkard and thief?

God also says in Proverbs 23:21 that by continuing to live as a drunkard you will become poor and miserable. "...for drunkards and gluttons become poor, and drowsiness clothes them in rags. Listen to your father, who gave you life, and do not despise your mother when she is old."

I'm pleading with you, my son, to stop and think about the direction in which your life is going. God says in Romans 8:7 the sinful mind is hostile toward God, and I am afraid that that is what I see in you. You have made yourself an enemy of God, and He will destroy you for the life you have lived and for your attitude toward Him. God has promised that if you stop fighting and agree that what He is saying about you is right; if you confess that you are a drunkard and a thief; if you lay hold of Jesus as the Person who died in your place—a drunkard and thief—He will forgive you for your sins and make you clean from everything you are guilty of.

This is a very simplified example, but the point is for you to see how a concerned Christian will convict you with specific actions, attitudes, and trends in your life, and show you specific Scriptures where God speaks about those things particularly.

Your Christian rescuer is called upon by Scripture to convict you himself by using Scripture, but he also relies upon the Holy Spirit to convict you (See 2 Timothy 4:2, John 16:8).

You may object to this idea of conviction, as many theorists have. They say, "The addict is already so burdened with guilt that if you further convict him of sin, he may fall into deeper despair. To convict him is not helpful, rather harmful." In response, I urge you to consider Revelation 3:19. Rather than bringing undesirable negative effects, conviction, as Jesus shows, is a very positive thing. Christ completely knows your heart and its misery. Yet in spite of that, he rebukes those whom He loves. This rebuke is exactly the same Greek word used in 2 Timothy 3:16 that is most appropriately translated "convict". Jesus convicts sinning Christians.

Why does Jesus do that? Why should your Christian rescuer do that? The all-important answer to both of those questions is because it is through this conviction that true repentance (*metánoia*) comes about. In conviction there is hope upon hope unspeakable that God will break into the dark recesses of your sinful heart and regenerate you with His life-giving power. Conviction brings about a sorrow for sin and a turning away from sin, which is accompanied by God's salvation. This is completely different from feeling bad in bad circumstances. It is a sorrow over the fact that you are not right with God. You have deliberately chosen to rebel against God and be His enemy. You have offended Him. You have used your body for your own selfish desires rather than for His glory. Through conviction is the hope of true repentance.

Chapter 7

THE TAME JESUS
DELUSION

IN OCTOBER 2003 the following story was reported in the newspaper. A couple went to camp out in a remote place.[21] He was an expert on wild bears and loved to film, photograph, and write about them. He would even approach them and touch them. While more cautious people would fear the boldness of this bear lover, he joked about their concerns. On one occasion a large bear knocked him to the ground and stood over him, but did no further damage. He considered the story amusing.

This trip, however, went horribly wrong. The only witnesses left to speak were the actual scene at the dishevelled campsite and the audio recording on the couple's video camera. The recording was a sick revelation of how it had happened. The ranger who listened to the track said that he was stunned by what he had heard. It was so disturbing that he kept hearing it in his mind. He found it difficult to distinguish between the noises made by the bear and those of the man.

The air-taxi pilot who arrived to pick the couple up could see a brown bear sitting on top of human remains and reported it to a local authority. In the camp, their video camera was found inside its bag with the lens cap still on. It appears that she must have activated the record function possibly by mistake as she leapt up in fright from her bed inside the tent. The first words heard on the audio recording carried a tone of surprise as she asked, "Is it still out there?" The six-minute recording repeated the sound of him being mauled by the bear, accompanied by her shrieking voice. He was shouting for her to hit the bear. She screamed, "Play dead! Play dead!" But shortly thereafter she began to cry, "Fight back! Fight back!"

The recording fell silent as the tape ran out. Both he and she were mauled to death in that camp. Their families were shocked.

If I had to ask you whether it is safe to pitch your little tent in a place where wild bears are known to live, surely you would agree it isn't. We have the evidence before us. In contrast, this couple were convinced that it was a calculated risk. They thought of the wild animals they were going to camp among and considered them tame enough to be so close to. They had domesticated those wild animals in their minds.[22] They felt safe enough to expose themselves to that danger.

In the same way, every day you go on pursuing your addiction, you feel safe enough to live in front of the face of God, who is a consuming fire, and pop just one more... You are comforted by a false comfort that God understands your rebellion, and He will be soft on you. He is a loving God and He won't call you to account for your lifestyle. He'll never condemn you for the way you have lived. Surely He understands the way you have justified your addiction in your mind. You were compelled to do it. If anyone else had been subjected to the upbringing, neighborhood, school experience, etc. that you were, they too would have fallen into the same addictions. It is a reasonable response in your mind. It also seemed reasonable to the couple in the story to pitch their tent in wild bear territory.

You may have padded your conscience with the idea that God is a God of unconditional love. He will accept you regardless of your way of life. David Powlison, in his booklet, *God's Love: Better than Unconditional* says this,

> If you receive blanket acceptance, you need no repentance. You just accept it. It fills you without humbling you. It relaxes you without upsetting you about yourself—or thrilling you about Christ. It lets you relax without reckoning with the anguish of Jesus on the cross. It is easy and undemanding. It does not insist on, or work at, changing you. It deceives you about both God and yourself.[23]

Don't be deceived by a casual attitude toward God and how He sees your lifestyle. Don't domesticate Him and treat Him as you would a house pet.

As you read these pages, you may be so trapped in your addiction that you see no way out, or you may be someone who is just flirting with your favorite sins. Whatever your story, if you are still pursuing a life of pleasant sensory experiences, your eyes are filled with things and people who, to you, are more beautiful and attractive than the lovely Jesus. You have found your affections drawn to the women on your favorite porn site, the thrill of being powerful, popular, or rich, or simply the pleasure of sleeping when you should be busy. Wherever your affections are, whether set on one object or habit or on many objects or habits, they are not set on Christ.

Regardless of this fact, it continually dazzles me how many people who live on the streets, begging for a living, appear to be so religious. They speak about God. They know the only way to be changed and put back on their feet is God. They tell you they are not angry toward God while at the same time acknowledge that it is His hand that has control over their circumstances. They know so much about God. They are so aware of the spiritual facets of their present condition. Maybe you are like that too. I can be writing to you in this vein, yet you already know most of my conclusions. You could be a very religious person.

But there is something missing from your concept of God. You have never experienced a passion for God. You have never experienced what it is like to be absolutely devoted to God in your heart where He is all you can think about and you must have a deeper relationship with Him. You have never been stirred by the glorious themes of the gospel. You have never been gripped in your inner being, finding yourself like John who saw the risen Lord and fell down like a dead man (See Revelation 1:17). You have never been like Isaiah who saw the Lord and cried out, "Woe to me! I am ruined!" (Isaiah 6:5). You have never been like Job, who after arguing his case and challenging God to answer him, called out, "My ears had heard of you but now my eyes have seen you. Therefore I despise myself and repent in dust and ashes." (Job 42:1-6).

If you honestly admit to the kind of "religious experience" you have been having, it is a casual, flat, domestic kind of thing that has no power. You have spiritual knowledge in the back of your mind, but it doesn't move you. Paul warned

Timothy in 2 Timothy 3:1-5 that terrible times would come in the last days. You might think he is speaking about huge wars and bloodshed, but he isn't. He was grieving over the time, which has now come, when people would have some kind of knowledge about God but be completely clueless about the saving power of God. In Paul's mind it is a tragic thing to live in a time when you can speak to anyone at random and find that they all have some knowledge about the Bible but have no power to live a life of personal holiness and Christian character. Does the knowledge you have of God drive you to your knees in confession of sin? Does the knowledge you have of God force you to abandon all your pleasant sensory experience gods to pursue the living God only?

You may care to know what the risen Lord of glory thinks of such a life—where you say you are a Christian, yet you have no power to excel as a Christian. In Revelation three, He speaks to the church at Laodicea. His eminent accusation is that those people have no heat, no passion, no life, no positive fire, or enthusiasm for God. He sees this kind of profession of faith with no pursuit of the glory of God as nauseating. He says in verse sixteen, "So, because you are lukewarm—neither hot nor cold—I am about to spit you out of my mouth." Where the NIV uses the euphemistic term "spit," the Greek word is actually far more graphic. It is a term of contempt that seems to be better translated "vomit".

Maybe you, like many addicts, have become fed up with the effort it takes to struggle out of a life of addictions and into a clean life of devotion to the Lord and have declared that you don't need this help. You can do it on your own. You can easily give up your habit by your own efforts. Sadly, you may be able to kick a habit on your own. Yes, you may have a strategy for sobriety. You may now be able to avoid the bottle store, whereas in the past you couldn't. You may be very proud of your achievement—you are no longer a drunk but a respectable, working person. Don't get me wrong. I really do think this is commendable, and it certainly brings an end to a certain degree of social misery.

What I want to tell you now, however, is that God wants more. God is not satisfied with mere sobriety. God doesn't want you to be like a drowned swimmer who has been pulled out of the water and now lies lifeless on the beach. No! He wants you not only to be pulled out of the water, but to be resuscitated, recovered, and to be the very image of radiant health. If all God wants for you is mere sobriety, He obviously doesn't have much in mind for you.

God wants your heart to be enraptured by Him. He wants you to know Him. He wants you to fear Him. He wants you to love Him. He wants all of these things for you in the most dramatically satisfying way possible. God wants you to be completely absorbed in breathtaking worship. God, the most desirable Being in the universe and infinitely beyond, must become in your eyes, in your heart, in your mind, in your emotions, and in your motivation bigger than anything or anyone you have ever known. God wants things for you that are still outside of your ability to grasp. He wants you infinitely higher than mere sobriety. He wants more for you than mundane existence as a "dry drunk." God wants you to be saved and sanctified.

This is why Paul shouts out, "Wake up, O sleeper, rise from the dead, and Christ will shine on you." (Ephesians 5:14). "Jesus Christ" is not the phrase you use when you realize you

THE TAME JESUS DELUSION

are begging from a Christian person and using His name will give you a better chance of getting something. "Jesus Christ" is not that comfortable concept you retain in the back of your mind like a safety net to fall back on when things get really hard. Jesus Christ is not a sleeping kitty cat on the window sill. He is the great lion of the tribe of Judah (Revelation 5:5). He is God almighty, creator and sustainer of the universe. He is the author of life (Acts 3:15). He is the great Savior. He is the judge of all men (Hebrews 12:23). Do not be deceived. God cannot be mocked. A man reaps what he sows. (Galatians 6:7). Abandon the idea that you can live as you please and use God as a convenience, always ready to pamper your whims. He will not be played with.

I call upon you now, even as your eyes slip over these words, to stop for a moment. Confess this sin to God. Confess to Him that you have lived a life marked by your pursuit of things you think will satisfy you rather than pursuing that which pleases Him. Confess to God that you are like the trapeze artist who flies high, soaring fantastically in the air, but who depends upon the safety net below in the likelihood of his fumbling a catch. Confess your sin of seeing Jesus as a person who will always continue to accept you regardless of how you live. Confess to Him that you see no beauty in Christ, only a vague religious idea that always niggles at your conscience. Confess that you would rather live a life of sinful pleasure than a life of personal holiness. Bow down on your knees before God, confessing these sins, and any others you are aware of. Ask Him to forgive you for your sins (See 1 John 1:8-10). Ask Him to accept the blood of Christ as payment for your sins because you can't bring to God anything that would commend you to Him (See Ephesians 2:8-10). Ask

Him to take away the filthy life of sin you are wearing like clothing, and ask Him to wash you clean in the blood of Christ and dress you in the wonderful new garments of Christ (See Romans 3:21-25, Philippians 3:9).

As you do this, you are making a new commitment. You are beginning a new life where you will begin to cultivate a passionate faith in the Lord Jesus (See 1 Thessalonians 1:9b-10). This new faith, the ability to see into the glories of the kingdom of God, will begin to affect everything you do (See 1 Corinthians 10:31). Deliberately lay down your favorite sins, let go of them in your heart, renounce them, and turn around to lay hold of the lovely Jesus. Without coming to Christ in this way, you have no hope of overcoming your slavery to pleasant sensory experiences.

This new life is a life of zeal. As Jesus was consumed with zeal (See Psalm 69:9, John 2:17), so you must be consumed with zeal for Christ both in your attitudes and actions. You have a colossal confrontation ahead and nothing less than devouring veneration for Christ will prepare you for the onslaught. Jesus too had a mission to accomplish—a mission that would take Him to the most extreme limits. He would achieve the objective set before Him by His Father. He would do it alone, in the face of gruelling opposition from every side. He would do it in a human body, deliberately restricting His use of divine attributes. He would subject Himself to the complete human experience and overcome as a man. He would endure inhumane torture and years of exposure to the elements. He would not aspire to greatness in this world even though He was and is God incarnate. He would have to deny Himself comforts and luxuries that we grab as necessities. Jesus was facing a mission no other man could ever possibly accomplish. By languishing over His stirring heroism, we come to understand something of what the Christian life is all about. As you begin your new life, let's reflect in the next chapter on how the great Savior faced His mission. We began with the story of how our campers underestimated the bears, in the next chapter we will continue with that analogy.

Chapter 8

UNIVERSAL HERO
MAULED

WITH THE TERRIBLE bellowing and thrashing of our camper as he fights for his life under that wild bear still in our minds, I would like to turn our thoughts to another critical element in the struggle against addictions. But before I do that, allow me to insert a quick note of acknowledgement. If you have heard Dr. Albert Martin's series of sermons on the passion of Christ, you will detect that they have deeply impacted my thinking in this area of worship.[24] I write this chapter with gratitude to the Lord for Dr. Martin's passion for Christ. In one of his sermons, he speaks of a picture he has that portrays the Lord Jesus as a baby in the manger with the shadow of a cross lying over Him. There lies God incarnate in an animal feeding trough in the cold draught from Golgotha.

The gospel is a story of deliberate action. Here the Lord of glory comes into the material world in a body prepared for Him, a body in which He would suffer the agonies of crucifixion (Hebrews 10:5, Isaiah 53:3). Jesus' life was to be a life of sorrow, poverty, and suffering. He came into our world as a servant, the Servant of Jehovah. (Isaiah 52:13).

Jesus' rejection, sorrow, and poorness, in contrast to ours, didn't come to Him as the consequences of sin—he had no sin (2 Corinthians 5:21, 1 Peter 2:22, 1 John 3:5). I see in Jesus a man who deliberately endured the kind of conditions that fallen human beings cite as the reason for their sin. A persistent addict, whose father had turned him out of the family home and refused to welcome him back, looked at me and said, "What does my father want? Does he want me to go and rob people to survive?" If you are familiar with that reasoning in your heart, or if you have heard it, you will hear what it is really saying. It is insisting that your unfortunate circumstances are driving you to sin, to smoke, to drink, to drugs, to adultery, or anything else you do. Surely Jesus' sinless-ness is evidence enough that it is not your circumstances that drive you to sin, rather, it is your personal yearning for sin that drives you to sin (James 1:14). This was the conclusion we drew from Candi's story.

Jesus grew up, not only in the "hood" where he was unpopular because of the convictions of his heart, but in a world that refused to accept Him (John 1:11). He was rejected, despised, and ridiculed (Isaiah 53:3). If ever there was anyone who could have used His sufferings as an excuse to get high, it was Jesus—but He didn't.

You chuckle and say, "But Jesus is God. He had the power to live a clean life." May I encourage you, when you have finished reading this book, to open up a good systematic theology manual and read about the humanity of Christ? Jesus was and is completely man. While He remains completely God, please appreciate the fact that He was made like His brothers in every way (Hebrews 2:17) in order to complete the mission of God for Him in this world (Hebrews 10:7, 9).

For Jesus to feel hungry was exactly what it is for you to feel hungry. For Jesus to be insulted was exactly the same as it is for you to be insulted. For Jesus to be cold, hot, wet, thirsty, tired, and grieving was exactly the same as it is for you to experience those things. God says He was tempted in every way, just as you are (Hebrews 4:15). The difference is that He didn't use the miseries He went through under testing, trial, and temptation as an excuse to sin. If you have ever tried to seriously withstand a temptation to engage in your favorite sin, you will understand the power in the character of Jesus as a man, a human being, just as you are a human being. The issues are the same. In the face of these hardships and easy ways out (Matthew 4:1-11), Jesus deliberately forged forward because He had work to do. He was absolutely determined to complete His mission.

As you toy with the idea of slipping into a porn chat group, do you have this resolve to stay clean? What is it going to take to rip you out of that mindset and set you sprinting on the road to personal holiness? Jesus forged ahead with unbounded sinless excellence. What character. What was it that lay before Him, that drove Him on through the inhumane circumstances of this collapsed world? What pictures of glory do you need to see to hurl you forward with such zeal?

Oh, the heaviness that began to sink down upon His loving heart as He contemplated the cross. In His human frailty, He drew His closest companions to His side to confide in them (Matthew 26:38). The words that slipped over His lips betrayed His distressed condition. The Lord was overwhelmed—overwhelmed with sorrow to the point of death. If you thought that sick feeling you felt when you were caught with another man's wife was the worst feeling on earth, you were wrong. Jesus was consumed with a horrific sorrow as He bowed before the unbearable, glaring fury of His Father. And while you thought of how you would escape the consequences of your sin, even by suicide, Jesus pressed further into the manliest display of heroism this world has ever seen. Falling with His face to the ground, He cried out in anguish to His Father. The contemplation of what lay ahead was dreadful (Luke 22:43). Yet, Jesus advanced into that horror with heroic earnestness. Have you ever experienced this kind of earnestness in your fight against sin?

Filled with a sense of desperation, He had to complete this mission. The load was enormous upon His trembling human frame, but He strode on through sweat, terror, and tears. The everlasting state of every human being rested upon this one man's actions on this day. Jesus was fulfilling the mission of God.

Ah, the insult as they laid hands on Him and tied Him up! This noble man was processed like a villain. In their uncaring grasp, He watched His closest friends filter away, leaving Him stark alone (John 18:12). Jesus was condemned by the disrespectful political suspicions of Herod and Pilate after being disdained and trapped by His own people, the Jews. Surrounded, as it were, by wild dogs, tearing at His flesh, the lovely Lord looked upon His dear friend, Peter, who had cursed and sworn that he had nothing to do with Him (Psalm 22:16, Matthew 26:72, 74).

No words can describe the ignominy of this scene as it unfurled as a testimony against my sinful heart and yours. The delightful Christ was stripped and flogged. Every moment will endure forever in all of its intensity in the mind of God (2 Peter 3:8). The blood of His only Son, whom He loved so dearly, was airborne in droplets from the vicious claws of His enemies, falling to the dirt as if valueless. Through the soldiers' punching and spitting; through their malicious tearing out of His beard; through their jeering; Jesus the man went on. Through the whipping and the flesh-tearing agony, He would not turn back. He would go on. He would not be defeated. He loved His Father too much. He loved the people for whom He was suffering too much (John 19:1ff, Matthew 27:27ff).

Seeing the immolated Son, disfigured yet still inexpressibly graceful in demeanour, ignited an eruption of wild screams for His blood. No suffering, no agony, or no cruelty should be spared on this man. Hatred spattered from the fangs of the mob—shrieking for barbarity, murder, and carnage! Their minds were grappling for the most shocking torture for the object of their disgust—crucifixion! (Matthew 23:23).

Suspend the animation for a moment. Walk in silence among these people. Look into each bloodthirsty, hate-filled eye. That's you and I.

"Ah!" you wail in the moment. "Give Him something for the pain." But there stood the mangled Lord of glory, moments before the extreme torture of His crucifixion, and He wouldn't touch the analgesic concoction pushed at Him (Mark 15:23). The soldiers offered it to Him, possibly more for their benefit than His. To nail a sedated man to the beams of a cross was considerably easier for them than to have to fight a terrified man. In all His majestic bearing, Jesus went down—a man. He would not fight. He would not thrash and scream as His flesh embraced those invasive nails. He was a man of character. Oh, for men of such Christlike character in our effeminate modern world.

Jesus insisted on being the sacrificed Lamb who took away the sin of the world completely (John 1:29, 36). He would be aware of every pang, every moment, to its fullest degree. He intentionally abandoned Himself like a lamb to the slaughter (John 10:11). This, in Dr. Martin's words, was majestic self-giving and self-restraint.

Stark naked before the taunting eyes of the world, the lovely Christ surrendered His once perfect body to the wood of His cross. There He lay as He gave up His arms and legs to be punctured by the nails from which He would shortly be suspended. On His head He wore the penetrating crown of my sin. Every click of your mouse on that porn site, every drag on your joint, every drunken stupor, every pursuit of illicit sex, and every damned lust in your heart and mine was the hammer that struck those nails.

Causing unspeakable agony, His executors shoved His cross into the air and dropped it into the hole from whence it would protrude. There He was left to die in agony. He was suspended between heaven and earth—no longer welcome on earth, yet condemned by heaven. There began the horror of the fight to breathe. Every breath becoming more and more painful as He pushed Himself up on His nailed feet, pulling Himself up with His arms just for a breath of air. Finding the pain too intense, He again slumped down until the urge to breathe became unbearable. On and on it went—hours of unutterable agony.

Yet in spite of the spattering blood and the tearing of His flesh, He wouldn't stop. He would endure. In the face of the horrors of crucifixion, He would go on. He refused to ease the pain and fail to accomplish the redemption He committed Himself to accomplish. All He needed to know as He forced

Himself forward in endurance was that this was the delight of His Father. He would do it. No new level of cruelty or pain was enough to override His passion for the mission of His Father. He was not enduring with a morbid resolve. His Father's delight was His delight.

In Luke 23:33 we see Jesus crucified between two criminals to make Him look like a common felon. By now it should be overwhelmingly obvious that Jesus is not ordinary. Jesus is the center of the universe, the center of the world, the center of time, the center of history. Jesus demands to be the passionate center of your life. You see His display of complete self-giving to the desires of God. This is what God desires of you. God refuses to allow you to continue in the cold, religious, domesticated kind of religion we spoke about in the previous chapter. God will not have you treat Him like a house pet in the same way our campers treated those wild bears. You saw the macabre consequences of their complacency. Rather, God desires worshippers who will worship Him from hearts that are overwhelmed with the privilege of serving the living God (John 4:24, Colossians 1:29, Hebrews 4:11, 2 Peter 1:5, 3:14). Jesus was completely prepared to face the wild bear of the wrath of God, to be savaged and mauled, and then to die.

Impaled in anguish, the dear Lord entered the next phase of His sufferings. As He hung there, the fearsome wrath of God overshadowed the sun, snuffing it like a spark. It descended in blackness upon the voluntarily trapped human frame on that cross. Closing in upon His solitary figure with immense speed, it burst upon Him with savage ferocity. The incensed terrors of God slashed and tore at the Savior with unrestrained force, bellowing with savage cries. God was thrashing His Son with the vast rage dammed up in His indignantly holy heart. Jesus must suffer to the end for every sin, blow after blow. He deliberately stared into the fiery blast and was consumed (Isaiah 53:10).

As Jesus, in the darkness, endured the smashing, crushing, unsparing rage of God toward sin, heaven was ablaze with blinding justice. As much as this pouring out of His jealous wrath on His own Son pained the heart of the Father, the Father was delighted in His Son. And, as Jesus cried out on the cross to His Father, the Father would not withdraw His hand (Psalm 22:1, Matthew 27:46, Mark 15:34). Why? Because as much as the Father wanted His plan of salvation accomplished, so the Son desired with all His heart to bear the wrath of God against the sins of His people.

No words can describe the infinite thrill of pride cascading through the heart of the Father as He witnessed His own Son enduring, holding out, and weathering to the end a burden that no-one in the universe but He could bear. The very being of the Father pulsated with bursting delight as he blasted out His unspeakable judgements on sin, and His Son absorbed it adoringly. Oh, the worship. Oh, the unutterable heights of joy that issued in tears from the eye of the Father as He adored His Son.

This is what it looks like when God judges sin. Here God is dealing with your sin and my sin forever. In deathly silence, the black beast retreated, permitting frightened fingers of sunlight permission to again explore. Reverent rays caressed the sad features of this sacred scene. They revealed a scene so ugly, yet so beautiful. Few eyes looked upon the mauled, smashed, grotesque contours of the once lovely Jesus. This is what it looks like when God judges sin. While this scene is ugly, it is simultaneously attractive beyond description. That should've been me. That should've been you. But in chords of love, God sees Him as me. God sees me as crucified with Christ. Does God see you as crucified with Christ? May these pictures never leave your heart, but grow to overwhelm you with love for Christ.

My aim in this chapter has been twofold—first, to extend my appeal to you from the previous chapter, to surrender to Christ. I desire your salvation. Second, I present Christ as the example for you to follow as you rise from your knees and follow Christ to a life of personal holiness. It is that life of personal holiness I would like to speak about in the next chapter.

Chapter 9

THE HOLY WAR

WHAT IS THIS stark reality upon which we have been staring in the last chapter? What you have just seen played out before your eyes is a kind of love—a love that is not simply a mushy notion; a love that is not simply a verbal commitment; a love that is not simply an emotion. You have seen a love that is sincere enough and strong enough to reach its goal. This is God's effectual love. When God created His plan of salvation, He knew that to accomplish it would cost Him more dearly than anything else in His entire existence. In Jesus we see a fiery love so strong that not even the most severe horrors and agonies in the universe could extinguish it. It is a love that reached its arm into the fire to rescue burning rebels (Luke 19:10).

Why did Christ do that? What outcome does He hope to bring about in your life? What was it that was so impressed on the heart of Christ that He would persist through all of *that* torture for you? One answer that should impact your life immediately is found in Ephesians 5:25-27. Here Paul is speaking about the church, the bride of Christ. He is comparing the way a husband ought to love his wife to the way Christ loves His church. Here the truth emerges that one of the reasons why the Lord Jesus persisted so heroically through the blast of God's wrath was in order to make the church holy. He gave Himself up for her, to make her holy. Although Paul continues to explain how this takes place, the point I am drawing your attention to is that if Christ had not given Himself up for His church, she would have been forever ruined.

Rather, what Christ achieved at Calvary has brought about a dazzling salvation. Not only is the bride of Christ rescued from the wrath to come, but she is made lovely in holiness. This comely holiness, in addition to her rescue from wrath, was the reason Christ gave Himself for her. It was this delightful beauty that fired His heart with passion as He endured the terrors of God's wrath. He could see her emerge with striking attractiveness out of the ugly ashes of sin and its consequences. In order to achieve this goal, the Lord Jesus pressed through hell—figuratively speaking. His passion was strong enough to power Him through that suffering in order to accomplish the end He desired.

I have labored the issue above because it is critical in your struggle against your personal sin. The thing you find more difficult to do than anything else on earth is the thing for which Christ has died for you. You find change the hardest thing in the world, but Christ died so that you can be enabled to change from the shame and misery of sin and its consequences. You no longer have to be a slave to sin.

You sense the struggle. You look at the necessary commitment looming above you like a foreboding tower that you have no hope of scaling. But God's agenda for you is change. Jesus desired your salvation and sanctification with such solemnity that He endured Golgotha in order to make them a reality in your life. Hold onto this truth in the face of popular psychology that shudders at this very thought. You must be transformed (Romans 12:2). God insists. Your lifestyle must change.

As you have read this book, you have encountered some shocking things about yourself. By nature you, like Candi, crave the filthy sins God hates. By nature you use your circumstances as an excuse for personal sin when in fact it is your lusting heart that desires and pursues your favorite sins—such a heart is not fussy regarding your reason for sin. So long as it is gratified, any springboard will do. By nature you wail over the miserable consequences of your sin without even a thought of true repentance—the metamélomai phenomenon. You don't see why you should feel remorse for something you love doing. You have hankered after God's things without yearning for God Himself.

If, in sorrow, you have seen yourself reflected in the pages of this book, you will acknowledge that your attitude is not much different from that of the soldiers who crucified the Lord. There at the foot of the cross, within earshot of Jesus' dying breaths, they began to divide up His clothes. They saw His things—His garments and shoes—but they didn't see Him. They didn't see God.

Is that you? Doesn't it tear into your heart to see these crass soldiers divide Jesus' clothes? Does it not gall you even more as you approach this scene in your mind's eye and see that one of these soldiers is you? Oh, that God would strike into your heart, even this instant, a dire hatred for that self-focused, things-attitude and bring you to your knees in repentance. "Oh, God, I have been blind to Jesus. All this time my mind has been consumed with the things I can get and enjoy and use, but my eyes have been blind to Jesus. Forgive me, Lord, for making myself and my desires the focus of my worship." Confess your sin to God—as I have been urging through these pages—and receive His forgiveness. This is the only way you can begin this journey of God-pleasing, achievable, personal change.

Even if you have responded to God in repentance as you have navigated this book—even at the beginning of your new life in Christ—a problem still remains. Your sinful habits are still deeply ingrained in your life, and you must now begin to do what you have never been able to do before. Do you see that just as Christ faced the terrors of the cross, you must face the overwhelming war you have been losing with your desires? Just as Christ endured the cup the Father gave Him to drink, so you must endure the struggles that lie ahead.

What I am saying is this, just as Christ demonstrated effectual love—a love strong and sincere enough to reach its goal—so you are going to need to exercise effectual love in order to reach personal holiness out of devotion to the Lord. In this, Christ is your perfect example. He has done it, and He has made it possible for you—empowered by His grace—to do it as well.

In spite of inevitable protests and objections, I would like, briefly, to show you how this change is going to take place in your life. If, as you have read these chapters, you have been born again by the grace of God, this is what your life is going to look like from this day forward.

Romans 6:19 encapsulates the thought when it says,

I put this in human terms because you are weak in your natural selves. Just as you used to offer the parts of your body in slavery to impurity and to ever-increasing wickedness, so now offer them in slavery to righteousness leading to holiness.

You will notice a pivotal phrase in this text that compares your old life with the new life you must now begin. The phrase is, "ever-increasing." Remember Candi? Recall how she began with sins that seemed quite harmless, but after a process during which her sins increased progressively, she found herself enslaved to her sins. She was trapped.

God is showing us what sin is like. You, and every other person who is trapped in sin, by nature slip into your personal sins progressively at a rate you feel you can handle. For a good illustration of this, consider the Ted Bundi story. He began flirting while he was still a child by catching glimpses of other people's adult magazines. With time, his desires became monsters that couldn't be contained. After a frenzied pursuit of his sins, he ended up on death row and was executed for raping and murdering many young women. Like him, you allow yourself more and more small sinful concessions. Eventually you are so emotionally involved with your sin that to break it off is like tearing off a part of yourself. Your sin is part of your identity. Without it you have no meaning or purpose in life. How did you get here? You descended into this state by slipping in, little by little.

It shouldn't be too difficult for you to conceive of a lifestyle that is exactly the opposite, should it? Paul says that in the same way that you clambered down into the deep dungeon of sin, step by step, so you are to climb out by the power of God. Just as you increased your wickedness in increments, so you must increase personal purity in increments. The struggle for personal holiness is long and hard, and the final stage is out of the reach of a beginner who desires to leap up there. Christ, however, has accomplished such a salvation for you that it includes the power you need to force you through even the hardest stages of the battle. Settle this in your mind for the long haul and be content with it. In God's agenda, your personal holiness is progressive.

You may simply prefer to live an "ordinary" Christian life. You don't feel the urge to become obsessive about personal holiness. You would rather simply depend on Christ's forgiveness when you sin and live in the same way everyone else does. You don't see yourself as a radical.

Please hear this urgent appeal. If this is the way you are thinking, you may not yet have realized the force of what I am saying. If you are a child of God, personal holiness must happen. You have no option. God insists. There is no other way. Take some time to think on the import of Hebrews 12:14 which slams down a chilling fact, "…without holiness no one will see the Lord." Every true child of God will see the Lord and delight in His presence forever (See this unbreakable chain in Romans 8:30). Therefore, every true child of God will become holy. If you console yourself with the thought of securing both God's salvation and your favorite personal sins, you are deceived. If you do not engage in the war for personal holiness you do not bear the family resemblance of the family of God. Just as Jesus pressed on through torment, so also you are required to set your heart and energies on the agenda of God for you—personal holiness (1 Peter 2:21ff, Ephesians 5:1-2).

Although this struggle won't be easy, it is entirely possible. What makes it possible is the final holiness Christ purchased for you on the cross. After true repentance, by God's grace, you must complete the mission that lies before you (Philippians 3:13-14). You must set out on the road to personal holiness and lay hold of the final goal—personal holiness—just as Christ set out on the road to purchase you for God and did actually do that—regardless of what agonies that mission required.

As our camper engaged in a death struggle with that wild bear, one thing he knew—it is not safe to give up. It is not safe to just lie there and play dead. You must fight. You must engage in the struggle. God will not permit you to continue, if you are His child, without a raging personal passion for the Lord Jesus Christ.

Chapter 10

THINGS ARE NOT
WHAT THEY SEEM

I T TRULY HAD been a wonderful evening at the Miss Teen pageant, and Lara was enchanting. She had stolen the hearts of the judges, the enraptured audience, and the new beauty queen to whom she had handed over her crown. Reaching for the final stretch of her teenage years, Lara had spent a glamorous year as Miss Teen.[25]

Michael, her father, was on his way to work in his car one morning, close to the end of Lara's year as Miss Teen, when he heard a radio DJ joking about his daughter. What he said was outrageous. Lara's father, a conservative pastor, knew that people like his daughter were bound to be the object of the world's scorn, so he planned to lay a charge against the DJ for spreading the rumor that his delightful daughter was pregnant.

Others joined the orchestra of gossip, including some of the photographers who had been at the event. They sniggered that she had looked a little "thick" around the waist on the evening she had handed her crown over to the next Miss Teen. Michael lived in the same house with his daughter. He saw her every day. There was no chance she could be pregnant. The fools who spread these rumors needed to be put into a position where they would have to publicly renounce their statements.

Lara's agent, a compassionate lady, was in the center of the tussle and took it upon herself to help by finding the exact source of these rumors. She knew it was a laughable suggestion that Lara could be pregnant, but to make a public show of the absurdity of the rumors, she asked her to go to a doctor to have a pregnancy test done. The test results came back negative, confirming her family and her agent's convictions; she was certainly not pregnant. In fact, she didn't even have a boyfriend.

In this case, the test result was negative. But let's suppose for a moment that the rumors had been true. Suppose she had become pregnant and had managed to conceal it for the full term of that pregnancy. Suppose it had been exposed that even though she didn't have a boyfriend, she had been involved in this extended, news-breaking scandal and deception. What would it have been like for her pastor father, her mother, her sisters, and her agent to look into her eyes and come to fully understand how she had deceived them over all of those months? Consider the heaviness of those moments—the clock ticking like thunder on the wall—as the truth is revealed. Suppose she had managed to pull something like that off.

The force of the impact as you suddenly realize you have been deceived is tremendous. You had no idea that the person you were speaking to was deliberately deceiving you. He seemed so pleasant, and you actually liked him. How could he possibly have been deceiving you? It is a terrible position to be in, to be deceived. You feel safe when you're not actually safe. You feel comfortable when you shouldn't. You let down your guard when you are most vulnerable, and suddenly, like a screaming bullet from a sniper rifle, it hits you. You have been deceived.

As you read this page, you may have your wits about you, and you are quite confident that you are able to discern who people are and what they are like. You feel quite safe that you know where you stand with your family, friends, and next-door neighbour. As you squeeze that sugar into your veins, you feel pretty confident that the character who sold it to you gave you what you paid for and not arsenic. You wouldn't be the first to be deceived in that way. You think you are sipping an ordinary Coke at the bar when in fact you are drinking Coke and undetectable Ketamine. The actual world and your actual condition are very different from your perception of the world and your perception of your condition before God. Beware! Things are not what they seem.

When I say that you are deceived, I'm not simply poking my opinion at you. God declares that everyone is deceived. Since the fall of man in Eden, not one human being has been able to think completely accurately. Sin has affected your mind. Your trusted thought processes are lying to you about reality.

Out of the myriad of things in which you are deceived, what is of critical importance, is that you are deceived about God (See Romans 3:11). This really is a life-and-death matter. Would you like to be blindfolded and told to walk straight ahead because it is perfectly safe and find that in the next second you are plummeting down the vertical face of a sheer cliff? No, you wouldn't. But that is exactly what is happening to you when you are deceived about God.

"What do you mean I'm deceived about God?" That's a good question to ask because it shows that you are unaware of how you could be deceived about God. Let me put it more specifically. In Romans 8:7 God says that the sinful mind is hostile toward Him. You begin life with bitterness toward God. You view him suspiciously and don't like what you think He is doing with the world and your life. This hostility is universal. Everyone demonstrates it (See Romans 3:11).

This means that if something goes wrong in your life, you will immediately look around for the cause and inevitably consider God to be the one in the wrong. You are dogged by a secret belief that God is not good, that He is vindictive. You secretly believe that God loves to flash temptations before your eyes that light the furnace of desire in your heart, but then He chuckles and holds you back, denying you access to what seems to be the epitome of delight. You clandestinely suppose that God loves to make you suffer and squirm under His almighty thumb, putting you in an impossible situation. You are convinced that God loves to watch you, gleefully smashing you down the moment you fall into sin. In your mind, God is unreasonable, and His standards are ludicrously high. This is the first area in which you are deceived. Beware! Things are not what they seem.

Woefully, this is not where the deception ends. While you consider God to be unreasonable, you simultaneously consider the things you crave to the point of frustration to be more desirable than God. You are convinced that there is something better out there than the things God offers you. You are persuaded that if you had to live your life completely for God you would lose out on millions of really good things in exchange for a dry, colorless life. If you are agreeing with at least some of the things I am saying, you can mark yourself as deceived about God.

This deception began at the dawn of time. Notice that this was Satan's lie from the beginning. He painted the picture so enticingly for Adam and Eve (Genesis 3:2-6) that they really thought they were missing out on something inestimably desirable. The lie you believe by default is that God is not good, while you simultaneously believe that sin is really good. Doesn't it stand to reason that because you are born in sin, sin is the most desirable attraction to your affections? Shockingly, Adam and Eve knew God but still believed the lie of Satan. Probably if you were asked whether you believed God was evil or good, you would say He is good because to suggest that God is evil is taboo. Even though you have that fragment of truth built into you, you still believe the lie that He is not good and sin is good. Beware! Things are not what they seem.

If you are a teenager who has grown up in a Christian home, you know all the facts you have been taught about God. You know all of the Bible stories and how God blessed the people He loved and punished his enemies. You know that God is the epitome of goodness and rightness—otherwise you would have no sense of guilt when you sneak around the corner to smoke in secret with your friends. But in spite of all of these things you know about God, you still have this nagging feeling that you can't give yourself wholly to God because if you did, you would be trashing the thrill of life. You are truly convinced that God simply wants to hold you back from all of the fun. As you look at the exciting prospects of getting out in a car with your friends, hanging out, raving, parties, music, clothes, image, sensuality, flirting, sex, drugs, food, movies, etc., you see those things as overwhelmingly bright compared to *God* who suddenly seems unbelievably dull.

Edward Welch's illustration pictures this frustration well. He speaks of Alcatraz prison. The prisoners could sometimes hear the sounds of free-life wafting across the waters of the San Francisco bay. They cursed the walls that separated them from that freedom. You are prone from birth to curse God, like those prisoners cursed their walls, for keeping you from the "good things" in life. You are deceived about God.

As you hand over your money and sit at that strip club staring at women who feed your lusts, you are demonstrating your true covert beliefs. You are exposing your true unspoken beliefs. You are declaring that in spite of the fact that God doesn't agree with what you are doing, you are convinced that there is enough reward for you here to compel you to disobey God. You believe the lie that in this place is something of real value that God is keeping you from. You don't see why God has to be so unreasonable, putting His foot down on things that are so delightful. Beware! Things are not what they seem.

Two years ago, a farm worker in our valley was cleaning out the harvesting machine after a long day's work. He and his crew had been harvesting butter beans from the fields. The harvesting machine was parked in the workshop with its mechanisms turned off. This worker saw that there were still a few beans lying loose in the end of the auger (a long corkscrew shaped blade that turns inside a tube to "pump" the beans out of the bin). He simply reached into the hole through the auger tube and began to scrape the loose beans out of the opening at the bottom.

Unfortunately, unbeknown to him, there is a sensor switch on the auger that senses whether the tube is empty or not. If it senses there are still beans in the pipe, it begins to turn to eject the remaining beans. As the worker pushed his hand into the little opening, the auger turned on and began to rip his arm up into the tube. As he began to scream, the machine operator came running, sprang into the driver's seat, and switched the auger off. By this time his arm had been cut right through in two places and warm blood was seeping out onto the workshop floor at an alarming rate. He was on his knees in agony with his arm jammed, above his head, in the auger.

What was he thinking? He believed the machine was harmless because it was switched off. He didn't take the automatic switch into consideration. He believed he could reach out his hand and safely scrape the beans out of the auger. He was wrong—just as you are wrong when you reach out your hand to that syringe, porn magazine, joint, pill, drink, or soap opera. Beware! Things are not what they seem.

In addition to the fact that you are deceived about God, you are also deceived about yourself. One man I counselled became very hostile when I told him how God sees him. He suddenly erupted and shouted that he was sick and tired of my telling him he was a sinner. He bellowed that it was unhelpful and was breaking him down rather than building him up. He couldn't hear any more and refused to be involved in counselling with me any longer. He was deceived about himself. He had the impression that he was a better person than God says he is. He knew he had sinned but was convinced that he was basically a good person. Except for a small handful of flaws, he considered himself quite acceptable to God.

We spoke earlier in this book about the Lord Jesus—specifically, about the poverty and unsuitable conditions in which he grew up. I spoke there about the fact that in contrast to how the Lord Jesus lived through those conditions and shone with moral beauty, you and I take those circumstances as an excuse for sin. Possibly you are angry with God for the circumstances you find yourself in. If you have been an addict for any length of time, you have certainly suffered the loss of many things dear to you. In your present misery, you may be pointing your finger at God, holding Him responsible for your bitter circumstances. After all, you felt obliged to sin in those circumstances. You console yourself with the fact that if anyone else had been in your shoes, they would have done the same.

You may consider yourself a basically decent person, but believe God has maliciously dealt you a bad hand, and now He insists you win the game. You shake your head at this image of God in your mind's eye because in your estimate, he is totally unreasonable.

Out of the volumes that could be written on this subject, let me simply respond to this lie by laying before you some evidence to the contrary. I fully agree that every tiny detail of your life has an impact on you. The environment in which you grow up impacts you. The language people use around you and the way they speak to you and treat you influence you. The media you are exposed to, the people who cross your path, every detail of your life has a profound impact on the person you will become.

Having said that, however, you need to arm yourself with the fact that although all of these details in your life have an influence on you, they do not determine the person you become. No circumstance is able to make you sin against the Lord. Sin is a deliberate choice you make. Regardless of your circumstances, they can never be blamed for your personal decision to sin. You personally make that decision when you face the opportunity to respond either in a sinful manner or in a godly manner. When you are about to order your first drink in the pub, it is not your circumstances that are making you sit there and drink. You have chosen, in those circumstances, to respond in that way. You have done so willingly. You take advantage of an opportunity where you know you are unlikely to be held accountable. No-one will know.

To see a perfect example of a person who was mistreated from a tender age and who, in spite of that mistreatment, insisted on doing what was right instead of what was wrong, consider Joseph in Genesis 37-50. In the face of overwhelming opposition, Joseph strode on in honor rather than slumping into sin. By far the most dramatic example in Scripture is that of the Lord Jesus, of whom we have already spoken.

God is more than reasonable. In fact, God has been overwhelmingly patient with the rebellious human race for thousands of years. This is what Paul is saying in Romans 2:4 and 3:25-26. The problem lies not with God but with your own fallen heart. Scripture says that you don't understand the world or your life from God's perspective (Romans 3:11). You are not able to focus on what you are truly like because your mind has been warped by sin. You are fortified with the estimation that while *you* are thinking clearly, *God* is unreasonable (Proverbs 19:3). Beware! Things are not what they seem.

Oh, if only you could see your true state of deception. If only you could see that you are diseased with sin beyond cure, falling to your death with no hope of rescue. If only you could see that you don't just need a plaster to cover a scratch, you need to be raised from the dead. If only you could see that you are dead in sin, spiritually blind, unable to see the glories of Christ or your own beggarliness. You are not generally acceptable to God with a few minor blemishes. Like your addiction, you are lost forever, without hope and without God in this world. No wonder all of your efforts to break the chains of your addictions have been as futile as washing a muddy pig with an earbud. What you need is a heavy rain.

The effulgent news to you is that the heavy rain is here. As you stagger, lost in the blackness, hear the dazzling news that God is presently reaching into fallen human hearts like yours and is inculcating the life of God into the soul of man. He is regenerating—giving new birth. For you, totally saturated with sin and craving filth, there is more hope than you can presently conceive. All the Israelites in the desert had to do when they had been bitten by a deadly snake was to look up at the bronze snake Moses had put on a pole. They looked at the snake as God had instructed them to, believing that as they looked, God was hearing their cry for mercy, and He would save them from the agony of death (Numbers 21:9). Look to Jesus and confess that you don't merely have a little scratch, you are moribund. Without Him, you have no hope. You have tried repeatedly to kick this habit, and you now realize that you are as good as in your grave. Jesus is your only hope. Look to Jesus and live.

You may argue that I have misunderstood you. You really are a nice person. You really are polite and kind. You wouldn't even dream of stealing from your own parents as so many addicts do. You have performed well in your studies and in your work. You are still healthy and helpful. In addition, there are many things I don't know about you personally.

106

You are right. There are many things I don't know about you. There is one thing, however, that I do know. From the list of things you could write about yourself that are good and commendable, not one of them is something you can claim to have sprung from your own good nature. In God's scheme, He has graciously lavished good things on all people, regardless of whether they are Christians or not.

Paul asks in 1 Corinthians 4:7:

> For who makes you different from anyone else? What do you have that you did not receive? And if you did receive it, why do you boast as though you did not?

It is God who graciously blesses you with all of the commendable features that make up your personality. It is God who gives you the ability to remain socially acceptable by your manner and restrains you from following your own evil desires into total corruption. You can't boast about your good manners or charm or intellect because every one of those things is a gift from God. Without God's gifts, you would be in the blazing fires of hell right now. He has given you more than you can imagine. Nothing belongs to you, only your sin, which God has graciously restrained until now. Look to Jesus in this helpless state and beg Him to have mercy on your soul. Beware! Things are not what they seem.

To sketch your predicament in even more macabre shades, not only are you deceived about God, not only are you deceived about yourself, but you are also deceived about the things you lust after. Regardless of whether you are a broken addict embraced in the arms of imminent death or whether you are still toe-dipping in the shallows of sin, one thing is sure. You are deceived about the sin you love.

You believe that there is something good for you in your favorite sin. If you lose this opportunity, you are losing something good. You believe that the window of opportunity is here and that if you don't lay hold of this lust right now, it will pass you by and you will be impoverished by not utilising it. This is the first lie. Every time you indulge in your personal addiction, you are making a declaration that you believe you are receiving something good.

You are also deceived about the objects of your lusts in thinking that they are harmless. You may protest and say, "I know my heroin is not harmless. It is killing me, but I can't stop." In response I say that every time you use, you declare your covert belief that your heroin is harmless. You don't inject it in order to die. You inject it in order to rush. If you knew that spike was going to be your very last, and the next thing your eyes saw in alarming sobriety was the fearfulness of hell, you would think differently about pressing that poison needle through your flesh and into your life-stream. Your actions betray your true beliefs.

You are emotionally attached to the object of your sin like a lover to his mistress. It is a secret, exciting affair filled with arousing intrigue. It is love. What beats in your heart as you hear the name of your first love mentioned is passion. The flame of ardent yearning blazes in your desires until you have gratified your lusts in her embrace. You must drink down more of the magic of your pinks or sleeping, slimming, pain tablets or ecstasy. It is not an unpleasant chore, you long to do it. This is what moves you, motivates you. "Just one more will be safe," you reassure yourself as you inhale from that crack pipe, *knowing*, but not *believing* for a moment, that this may be the final drag before your lungs go into paralysis. Your "harmless" god gloats as you gasp in the violent twilight of death.

You must realize that these things are outside of God's design for human life and are thus not safe! You and I simply presume we will be safe before God like the fool whose heart turns away from the living God. In Deuteronomy 29:19 he thinks, "I will be safe, even though I persist in going my own way." You think, "I can do this one more time. I can handle it." "You fool!" said God to the man who was thinking only about his own comfort and wealth without seriously considering God. That very night, his life was demanded from him (Luke 12:20).

This addiction is like a love affair. In the movie, *The Shining*, there is a scene where the main character is seduced by a woman in an abandoned hotel he has inherited. Day after day he follows her eerie form and eventually slips in through a bathroom door she has left opened for him while she showers. With heart pounding, he peers around the end of the door and sees her in a most seductive mood. Having fallen hungrily into her welcoming arms, he catches a glimpse of the two of them through the steam in the mirror. To his horror, he sees that while this woman appears delicious in the front, she is actually a rotting corpse at the back! Aghast, he tears himself out of her embrace, thrusting her away from him. All her luscious beauty has decayed in an instant. He sees her accurately for the first time—she is a cackling, decaying cadaver! He was every bit as deceived about her as you are about the object of your lusts. Beware! Things are not what they seem.

Many Christians have made a chilling discovery. Even after they have fought a long bloody battle with their sins, their old sins can still come back to haunt them. They may have been clean for years, and suddenly an aroma, a color, a song, a texture will bring a flood of longing memories of their old lover back to them in full force. That seductress desires them and is calling for them. She is waiting behind that open door for them to lust after her beauty.

You must uncover her deception and see her for what she really is. You must see that glass of alcohol as a glass of venomous spiders that you are about to spill into your throat. You must picture that secret lover as the wild bear that tore our explorers apart earlier in this book. You must see that little tube through which you are snorting your coke as a shotgun barrel, and you are tapping the trigger. Don't be deceived about your gods. Although you love them, they don't love you. Although you will preserve them and pamper them and sacrifice for them, they will not do any of these things for you. They desire for you the most miserable death possible. Beware! Things are not what they seem.

God is your judge. He is fully aware that Christ is not your first love. He knows completely the longings of your heart and the intensity with which you desire them. He watches you yearning deeply for release in the arms of a corpse who appears beautiful to you. He sees that your heart is not like that of Paul whose heart pulsated with passion for Christ who loved him and gave Himself for him. He has permitted you to pursue your lover and then to reap the galling consequences of that pursuit. You have received God's grace in inestimable ways since birth—life, health, faculties, shelter, clothing, food, society, family—yet you have chosen to disregard His beauty and chase after an illicit lover. Your heart is not moved by God's grace. You do not love the truth.

I appeal to you as you read this page, lay hold of God. Learn to hate what God hates, and learn to love what God loves. Become passionate about God and passionate about hating sin. You have seen the hatefulness of sin. Now learn to hate it as God hates it. It is not harmless. Beware! Things are not what they seem.

Let me tell you how the story ended. Lara's father was irate concerning the rumors spread about his daughter and threatened to sue the radio DJ who was spreading them.

Shortly after the coronation of the next beauty queen, Lara was found giving birth to a baby on the bathroom floor in her parent's home. What a shock, as they heard her distressed groans from behind the closed door, and in an instant, learned the truth. They had been deceived. "But what about the doctor's certificate?" you may ask. She had taken care of that too. She had gone to a doctor who didn't know her and had handed another girl's urine in as a sample for the pregnancy test—obviously she tested negative. Everyone was stunned.

In a case where so many people felt absolutely certain that the stories of her pregnancy were just rumor, the truth came home with devastating force. May the truth of your three deceptions come crashing down on you with equal force as you turn the content of this chapter over in your mind. Beware! Things are not what they seem.

Chapter 11

SCREAMING AGAINST
YOUR LUSTS

NOT ONE. NOT two. No, it took twenty-five policemen to establish that a crime was in progress...," commented a reporter in a case where the police were sent on a mission to establish that illegal activities were taking place at two local strip clubs. While the law governs what acts may and may not be permitted in such clubs, actually charging the owners of such clubs with specific crimes turns out to be a little more difficult. The mission of these policemen was to enter the two clubs, blend in with the crowd, and then secure the sexual services of one of the girls in exchange for money. If they could do that, they could prove that the owner of the club was guilty of such practices under the law.

Although all of the policemen were on the same mission, it took a very junior officer to detect this criminal activity. How could a mission such as this be so hard? The answer to that question was well encapsulated by one of the officers at the court hearing, "Sir, there were enough naked girls to divert anybody's attention."[26] You may be shaking your head in disbelief that twenty-four policemen were so distracted by the sights and sounds in the club that they couldn't keep their minds on the one simple mission for which they were there. This same officer said, "My attention wasn't there."[27] Something had so absorbed all of their attention that they simply couldn't focus on the mission intently enough to complete it.

In the same way, in this world, you are distracted from the mission of God by the overwhelming appeal of your favorite sins. Scripture is not blind to this reality. Quite to the contrary, Scripture openly declares that there *is* a degree of pleasure in sin. In Hebrews 11:25 we see a snapshot of Moses, like those policemen, with the pleasures of sin (the dancing girls) on the one side, and the mission of God on the other. As he evaluates the pleasures of sin, he is more overwhelmed by the awe of God and the grandeur of His mission. What these policemen experienced in that club is a universal syndrome, which has persisted throughout history. It is nothing new.

It is the appeal, this pleasure, which makes sin such a deadly attraction. The fact is, whoever you are reading these words, you are attracted to sin like those policemen were attracted to the dancing girls. The issue is not "if" but "what". The things toward which you are attracted are unique to you, but as a fallen sinner, there is something in your heart that yearns for sin of a certain kind. The more you indulge in your favorite sin, the more it gains control of your affections. Sin is like a lover to whom you are so deeply devoted that you could never dream of leaving. But at the same time this lover is engineering your death. It is a deadly attraction.

Pieter Mans, in his book, *Drugs*[28], cites a boy named Stephen saying,

> It has now been eight weeks since I left the rehabilitation center. At school I experimented with dope, ecstasy, acid, and coke, but nothing gave me the rush everyone was talking about. During my first year at varsity a friend introduced me to smack. When heroin is injected in your veins, you experience an overwhelming rush in your body and your mind. After that, your body relaxes and you instantly feel totally at peace. It is an amazing experience.

He says a little further on, "I can't imagine not ever using drugs again."

Are these not the romantic longings of a lover, the fond yearnings of an addict for the pleasure of his sin? These hankerings are exactly what take your mind off the mission. They divert you from the very purpose for which you even exist. Surely I need not elaborate any further. It is because of these out-of-control cravings that you are even reading this book at all. You are faced with the universal, overwhelming appeal of sin. Where is your attention?

To add to this predicament, you have also surely discovered that not only are you dogged by your longing for your particular habit, but you are also crippled by your own lack of self control. You lack the ability, described by Edward Welch, to cultivate the skill of living a thoughtful, careful life in which you do what is right despite your desires. You lack the ability to exercise this self-control especially when you are alone or feeling dissatisfied. You become a ravenous beast when no-one is looking. Don't you long for a principle settled so deep in your inner being that in *those* situations you will not be ruled by your sinful desires—the dancing girls—but by what God desires for you? Self-control, says Welch, is the skill of saying "no" to sinful desires, even when it hurts. Is this a thing you wish you had?

You have tried to pretend your desires aren't there—ignoring them and hoping they will just go away. You have tried simply saying "no." You have tried to exercise self-control even in a small thing like sticking to a diet, getting some regular exercise, or trying to get out of bed earlier, but have failed.

Pursuing self-control in this way, meeting only with failure upon failure has instilled within you a deep conviction that there is something more to your hankering after your lover than plain and simple biology. The more you struggle to control the habits to which you are now enslaved, the more you know with certainty that there is something far deeper involved than just hormones and physical composition. You are distinctly aware of a complex body and mind interaction. Your mind sees your sins as unparalleled in desirableness, while your body responds with the thrill of the chase—again. There is an undeniable, unexplainable attachment in the most secret part of your being that drags you relentlessly toward wrong habits that are uniquely attractive to you personally. This is a deeply emotional thing.

This object of your lusts seems to you to be the very reason why you exist, and it seems insane to hold yourself away from something you love so deeply. The question plagues you, "Why can't I just do it if I love it so much? Why do I have to control myself?" While agonising over this, you find another principle at work. Even though the pleasure of this sin appears so desirable, one unfortunate downside is that the pleasure doesn't last indefinitely. It is not long before you must have just one more shot; just one more snort; just one more strip show; just one more click—because one fix has such a short lifespan. Moses understood this. The pleasure of sin is painfully temporary (Hebrews 11:25).

The cycle begins, fuelled by the desire for just one more. The first one tastes like just one more. Again, you discover something appalling. As this wheel begins to turn and you have just one more, after just one more, because the thrill is so short-lived, you realize that with each "one more" you find less satisfaction. It is like bailing water out of a boat where more and more water is flooding in all the time and the bucket you are using has a hole in the bottom that grows bigger and bigger with every scoop.

Colossians 3:5 describes this lifestyle in one word—greed. Your life at this stage is characterised by an eager desire for more. Every time you have had more, your desires have screamed for more in a never-ending cycle. Again, this cycle is pictured in Ephesians 4:19 where Paul speaks of people who give themselves over to sensuality so as to indulge in every kind of impurity with a continual lust for more. Once caught in this cycle, you can tumble into the depths of hell, out-of-control.

As if this is not bad enough, not only do you see your sin as overwhelmingly attractive; not only are you painfully aware of your own lack of self-control; not only do you discover that your sin only satisfies you for a short time; not only do you discover that after the satisfaction wears off you immediately want more, but you also discover the horrific truth of Romans 6:19. Every consecutive time you desire just one more, you are exhibiting the signs of being trapped in a cycle. With every rotation, that cycle demands something bigger and better than before. This becomes a principle. Not only do you indulge more and more in your particular sin, but you also find yourself indulging in sins that are greater than the sins with which you began. Now you not only smoke a joint but you want to smoke some buttons too. What's next? Crack? Smack? More than that, as you know, as your budget requirements grow, you are forced to make ends meet. Your sin is growing. Now its not only your habit that has you enslaved, but also the sins required to steal, deceive, cheat, sell, and manipulate yourself into a cash flow. At what point will you stop? Are you able to stop in this cycle? I think we both agree. You are enslaved, and your self-control has not been able to extract you until now. Scripture, you see, does understand this escalation—slavery to impurity and ever-increasing wickedness.

You are like a little man walking on a huge sports field in an enclosed arena. Your lusts are seated in their tens of thousands to cheer you on. There before you, appears the sin that turns your knees to jelly. Breaking out into a sweat, you pluck up the courage to say, "No." Swallowing the lump in your throat, you hear a gentle chant beginning to stir in the breathlessly quiet arena. It whispers at first, "Do it. Do it. Do it." You need no provocation, and you strengthen your resolve to remain pure. The chant grows louder, and very soon it surges to the deafening pitch of millions of screaming freaks. You can't take it anymore. Reaching to lay the soft palms of your hands on the one your heart loves; you pull back and are filled with an overwhelming urge to shout, "No!"

Filling your lungs and bellowing into the howling mob of your lusts, you yell with all your might, "*No!*" The crowd falls instantly silent, staring at you in disbelief. Unfortunately, their insane chorus falls away before you have finished screaming your protest, leaving you small and alone in the center of the arena. Instead of the roar, you thought was blasting from your soul, you hear a little squeak from a heart that really wants to stop, but is still too much in love with this overwhelming attraction before you. The baby-like gurgle that emits from your lips as a form of protest echoes in ridiculous tones, tinkering with the emptiness. Another roar explodes from your jeering lusts—laughing you to scorn. You can't do it. You are feeble. Give it up and smoke the thing. Sleep with her, you fool! They shout you into submission as you fold yet again into the arms of your lover.

You have learned that just saying "no" is a hopeless exercise. It is not enough to smash the power of your raging desires. The attraction of your sin is diverting your attention from the mission for which you exist. Your life is not meeting your Maker's specifications and purposes. In this state, you soon become aware of another sickening truth that thumps down on your conscience. Attached to this lifestyle are consequences that suit the sin. You are swept into sin, powerless—out of control. It is a hateful cycle, round and round it goes, deeper and deeper into the agony of separation from God.

By now you may be asking this question, "If I crave my particular sin with all my heart, and my best resolve, in the face of the attractiveness of my sin, is not enough, is there still hope?" The answer is an overwhelming, "Yes!" We will now consider a breathtaking kind of beauty that is fully capable of absorbing your complete attention forever.

Chapter 12

GRINNING WITH A BELLY FULL OF KNIVES

THERE WAS ONCE a little boy who loved to eat. In fact, he loved to eat so much that he often ate too much. He used to eat huge quantities of food, loaded high on his plate. He would eat at mealtimes and at any time in-between. He would eat anything he could lay his hands on. Now when I say anything, I mean that he really did eat the strangest things. He knew there were some things he probably shouldn't have eaten, but he had eaten them because he really wanted to. After all, no-one would know about all of the things he had eaten.

This little boy grew up and became a man. He became very fat because he was still eating everything he wanted to eat. Not surprisingly, he began to feel very sick. When he went to see a doctor, the doctor told him he shouldn't eat so much. The man really wasn't feeling very well, so he took his doctor's advice. Although he didn't eat as much anymore, he continued to eat some things he knew he shouldn't. How was the doctor going to know he had eaten those things anyway?

The time came when he was in so much pain that he had to return to his doctor. When the doctor felt the man's abdomen, he could feel a large hard lump in his stomach. It was a very strange lump, so the doctor told the man he would have to operate. Very frightened, the man eventually consented to the operation and was wheeled into the theater. To the amazement of the doctors and theater staff, they discovered what the huge lump in the man's stomach was. They removed more than 300 coins, including quarters, dimes, nickels, pennies, and subway tokens. They also removed broken thermometers, can openers, knives, forks, spoons, nuts, bolts, chains, and car keys.[29]

He thought no-one would ever know he was popping a can opener into his mouth or a set of car keys. Unfortunately, with every indulgence, his problem increased until he could bear the pain no longer. The thrust of this story is that this man failed to control his desires to the point where he stopped himself from doing something foolish and harmful. It was self-destruction, just like every other form of lack of self-control. As an addict, you know this predicament. You know that your habit is destroying you, like that man swallowing the odd knife and thermometer here and there, but you fail to exercise enough control over your desires to steer clear of calamity.

After struggling with self-control for such a long time, you may even have given up altogether. If this is the case, I would like to encourage you in this chapter to begin on a new journey to honorable self-control. I believe you can do this because every true child of God has the Spirit of God living in him. When He takes up residence in a child of God, the Holy Spirit produces fruit in that person's life that speaks of His presence. One of those fruits is self-control. As you pursue self-control

(1 Timothy 6:11[30]), the Holy Spirit causes it to grow. But before you begin to pursue self-control, let's answer the question, "When God is asking you to urgently pursue self-control, what is He asking you to pursue?" Do you have the right picture in your mind when the term "self-control" is mentioned?

Paul concludes his list of the facets of the Fruit of the Spirit in Galatians 5:23 with self-control. No-one would disagree that in order to cultivate any of the previously mentioned facets of the Fruit of the Spirit, you are going to need a lot of self-control. It appears that self-control is a facet of the Fruit of the Spirit that is included in the development of all of the other facets. It is not going to be easy to change from living a life of self-absorption to a life where you love other people. You are going to need to exercise real self-control to be joyful even in circumstances that make you want to scream. It is going to take work for you to deliberately relinquish your heart-burdens into the capable hands of the Lord, and then thank Him for taking them, refusing to allow them to worry you anymore. The same can be said of all of the elements of the fruit in Galatians 5:22-23. Self-control is necessary no matter what facet of the fruit you begin to cultivate. Therefore, you are never wasting your time when you work on self-control.

Maybe you consider self-control outside of your capabilities right now, and if you have not yet committed your life to the Lord Jesus as your Master, you are right. It is outside of your capabilities. For the child of God, however, self-control is not an elusive notion, but a developing reality, even a command. God expects self-control from everyone, regardless of who you are.[31] The fact that you are not yet born again doesn't release you from this obligation. God's standards hold for all people, and all people will be judged according to what they have done (Matthew 16:27, Romans 2:6, Revelation 20:12-13). God's salvation through Jesus Christ is your only hope and the only starting point to a life of self-control.

Lack of self-control is well described in Ephesians 2:1-3, a text any addict should be familiar with. Lest you fall into the trap of considering yourself unique in your lack of self-control, notice that everyone has to fight the battle to gain self-control. Verse three says that all of us lived without self-control at one time. All of us gratified the cravings of our sinful natures. All of us folded to our lusts over and over again. All of us were bound to the maddening lusts in our thoughts, feeling compelled to obey them. Those who continue to live like this remain objects of God's wrath. Development of self-control as a child of God is your only hope.

Having said those things, let's continue to answer the question already posed, "What is self-control?" The Greek term translated "self-control" in English is the word *egkrateia*. It comes from the Greek word *kratos* which means *power*. So to have self-control is to exercise power or restraint over your own impulses and desires. Self-control means self-command. It is to be the master of what you want. Too often, self-control is seen as controlling the depth to which you indulge in the things you desire. Rather, understanding it correctly, self-control is the facet of personal character that exercises control over what you actually desire.

Having gone this far, another fact is obvious. Once you have understood that when God is asking you to cultivate self-control, He is asking you to cultivate the ability to control your desires, you will naturally begin to look for a reason to engage in this war. No change comes easily. You are going to need huge fuel for your motivational furnaces in order to pursue self-control. This is simply because your desires are such a powerful driving force in your life and folding to their demands has already dragged down huge calamity on your head. Motivation is a colossal factor in your struggle for self-control.

You may protest that there are certain things you really consider desirable, why can't you simply enjoy them? You may perceive this self-control thing as just another occasion on which you are ending up with the short end of the stick. You are being cheated. You will find yourself squashed between the commands of your desires and God's command to control them. Your desires scream in your heart while the voice of God thunders. In your outrage and under such pressure, you want to scream, "Isn't there another way? Can't God just inject some kind of personal power into me, because I feel too feeble to fight for it?"

If you know this struggle, you will agree with Thomas A. Kempis who said, "No conflict is so severe as his who labors to subdue himself."[32] This conflict, you must know, is not news to God. It is because of the raging sinful desires in our hearts that He insists on self-control at all. He knows you don't need to practice lack of self-control but its opposite.

We have already established the fact that a child of God is able to develop self-control. To know you will succeed, before you even begin, is a motivation from the start. But before I make some suggestions as to how you can start, let's consider what else you will put into the furnace of your motivation to self-control.

Have you ever been outraged by something someone has done and afterwards you discovered that they were actually doing something very nice? For example, someone has been acting suspiciously around you, like my wife did on one occasion. There was all this whispering and secrecy. You realize that when you walk into the room, it gets really quiet and when you leave, the laughing breaks out again. You begin to imagine what is going on, and you don't like it. They are talking about you behind your back, and you are the joke of the gathering.

I discovered soon enough that what I had thought was going on wasn't even close to what was actually going on. They had been arranging a surprise birthday party for my thirtieth. Was I surprised when I arrived and found numerous family members and friends gathered to wish me well for the next thirty years. My whole perspective changed. No longer was the secrecy veiled in the grim tones of deception, but in the bright colors of beauty. They had been planning something special for me with good intentions toward me.

It is exactly the same when you struggle with self-control. You may be very suspicious that you are losing out on real value when you have to master your desires. Meanwhile, the exact opposite is true. As you develop self-control, you are coming into God's true, wonderful riches. He is not being unreasonable. He is not hoping to make your life miserable. He is not trying to make you lose out on something of real value. God is bringing you into true value and blessing beyond your conception. Don't conclude that your negative interpretation of your struggles with self-control is in fact accurate to truth. They are not. What you need is a new clear perspective.

Exactly as we would expect, there is a word in the New Testament that speaks of this precise thing. It is the word *sophron*, used in Titus 2:2 (among other places) to mean *self-controlled*.

This is a fascinating word to consider in more detail. In Mark 5:15 it is used of a formerly demon-possessed man—an apparent lunatic—who was now in his right mind. It refers to a person who is thinking clearly with a correct perspective. Paul uses it in Romans 12:3, translated into English as sober. Contrast the way in which an inebriated person thinks to the way in which a sober person thinks.

So the call to be self-controlled is not only a call to be the master of what you desire, but also to think clearly and accurately. Thinking in this way, you will never be tempted to conclude that God is being unreasonable by insisting you hold yourself back from desiring things that are destroying you. To be self-controlled in the *sophron* sense is to be of sound mind, intellectually sound—without illusion, restrained, disciplined, or sober.[33] In this way you will see self-control as a privilege, rather than a curse.

If, in your desperate struggle for self-control, you knew there was a perfect reason why you should continue in your struggle, if only you could perceive it, would you not set your mind to discovering that reason? If you could see the rich blessings of self-control in the way God sees them, would you not be more motivated to pursue it?

It is this clear perspective God is calling you to in His Word. You need to begin to identify your personal sinful desires and think them through. See how your sinful desires and their seeming attractiveness are not actually positive blessings at all, but killers in disguise. We spoke about this in chapter ten—things are not what they seem. Your lusts are deceptive beyond description, just like the deception that drew our man to eat just one more knife. His lust was deceptive. It led to his destruction, not to his blessing. Just because you are experiencing difficulty finding a reason to continue, that doesn't mean there is no reason. The reason is there. You just can't see it yet.

What's so terrible about this deception—that your lusts tempt you with "good" things—is that it works in the opposite way too. This deception relentlessly drums into your mind the message that Christ and eternal glory are lifeless, dull, and boring and are not worth laying hold of. Your lusts deceive you into thinking that you are losing something valuable if you exchange your immediate passion for Christ and heaven forever. Your lusts will assure you it is worth the gamble. Your sin would love nothing more than to see you swallow that final knife, make that final decision to spike just once more, and watch you tumble into eternal misery. They would have achieved their goal—ruining your soul forever, beyond remedy.

You are filling your lying belly with knives, forks, spoons, nuts, bolts, and chains simply because you desire to eat them— but, you are simultaneously damning yourself. You have fallen for the lie. You need to begin to see accurately (*sophron*) before your lack of self-control (*egkrateia*) sinks you into ruin forever. You need to halt this mad rush toward your own doom. In the next chapter, I would like to show you the ultimate motivation for self-control. This is something you simply must see.

Chapter 13

COMPELLING
LIQUID BEAUTY

SLIPPING TOWARD THE beckon of gravity, it dribbled downward, embracing and coating with rich residue the crevices and splinters in its path. Teeming with tender, nourishing life, it now lay exposed on dead wood under deadly rays. How it glistened, arrayed in deep red beauty, reflecting monumental surroundings that spoke volumes—more than can be captured in words. This one droplet reaching for the sand, shouted the mighty cosmos still as it trickled from the Savior's hand. As the darkness stole away, permitting the dazzling light of day, reflect back to see this compelling liquid beauty.

In this blood are mysteries without number. From this blood screams an intense passion, sounding through eternity. A passion that sees this man, God incarnate, thrashed and mutilated to death. Vicious torture has brought Him to the grave with my face forever imprinted upon His heart. Thus shouts this compelling liquid beauty. Here is ultimate motivation.

Through the ages, this blood has cried the most intimate thoughts of God to man. It opens the way to hope and glory, blasting open the gates that imprisoned the wicked. Desperate people can now be washed clean in this blood-red flow of compelling liquid beauty. For ever and ever I'll beam brilliant white before God in ecstasy beyond description. As it shrinks and dries, this drop shouts this and more, more and more, for ever and ever and ever.

Still today, in this present age, this blood still shouts out the thoughts of God; the passion of His heart; the cleansing of your sins; and the promise of glory unfathomable. In this modern age, you may wonder how this blood still speaks. Your life is filled with things that seem so far removed from the idea of cleansing blood. You're struggling with coke or smack or porn in an age of modern convenience, not in a cultic world of religious ritual. Allow me to share with you the ultimate motivation for the struggle you face if you are going to know any degree of freedom in your present life and reward in the life to come.

God knows about the present age.[34] God knows fully the hellish desires in your heart. He knows the temptations that smash away at your resolve, hour after hour, moment after moment. He knows the burden of guilt you bear, riveting you with the agony of worry and restlessness and depression. He knows it is almost impossible for you to remain unaffected by the lust and desire upon which the world builds its system, and that you are uniquely susceptible to your own personal flavor of sin (chapter two). God knows.

In spite of your hard experiences, there is nothing you can tell God that would make Him blush. He knows where you have been; what you have done with whom; what you were thinking; what you desired; what your motives were; why you were driven by those motives at that time. He knows all of these things and infinitely more about all of the people, all of the time, throughout all the world, and all history. God understands your life more fully than you do. He understands the way your computer works, your programming tricks, and all the jargon. There is no mystery in you or in this present age that constitutes a mystery to God, everything lies naked in front of His piercing eyes (Hebrews 4:13). No modern mind can conjure up a more up-to-date, trendy image of the sophisticated age in which we live than the accurate perception of it in the mind of God. God in fact smiles at our infantile discoveries, releasing more knowledge to the human race whenever He desires. You are a creature of time, you age, you become out of fashion and outdated with all of your ways and things, but God surpasses time. God rules time and uses it to serve His purpose. God surpasses technological breakthroughs. He is the epitome of sophistication.

My point is that God understands the whole system of which you are a part in every microscopic detail. And in this present age (Titus 2:12), God has provided you with instruction on how best to escape and remain free from your addiction. No technique this world has ever concocted can, in its baby-like stature, ever match the deep wisdom of what God has to teach you about how to deal with your cravings. You would be wise to relinquish what you consider wisdom and hear what God has to say. To fail to do so is to oppose the wisdom of God and to expose yourself to the miserable consequences of your folly forever. To know that God completely understands your present circumstances provides huge motivation.

What are you doing right now? What are you doing with your life? God says you are waiting (Titus 2:13). You may be like the man in Bruce Springsteen's song who was sitting around waiting for his life to begin, while it was all just slipping away. You could be waiting for anything, but ultimately, you are either waiting for Christ to return (or your death, whichever comes first) or to be admitted to the unspeakable horrors of hell. The children of God, while they live and struggle against personal sin, are waiting in expectation as a person waits for a friend they haven't seen for a long time. Christians are excited, filled with a sense of anxious anticipation, because Christ will appear at any moment. Joseph of Arimathea, who went boldly to Pilate who had condemned Jesus to death, was a man who was waiting for the kingdom of God (Mark 15:43). He was longing with joyful anticipation to be received into Christ's eternal glory, and he is there right now. For him, the long wait came to an end, and he has already been in the blazing presence of God for two millennia. To know that life in this fallen world will not meander aimlessly forever is immense motivation.

If you are a child of God, you are waiting for the blessed hope (Titus 2:13). Something so extraordinary looms ahead of you that when you are enveloped by it, you will be completely satisfied at last. It will be something so wonderful that it will entirely change your whole being and surroundings. You will be snatched from this corrupt, decaying, temporary, miserable sphere of life, leaving it behind as a distant memory. This blessed hope will most certainly come upon you and is, even now as you read this page, rushing toward you at an immeasurable speed. It will transform you. It will free you. It will so elevate you and expand your mind and senses that you will not be able to compare your renewed state to anything you have ever experienced in this fallen world. To know that your life will not just fizzle out into blackness, but will explode into brilliant new life is outstanding motivation. You are living toward a certain hope, not inevitable defeat.

Not only will the coming of this blessed hope be a thrill to experience, but while you wait, the tingle of excitement mounts in anticipation. You find delight even just thinking about it. It consumes your life with joy regardless of your circumstances. Finding daily joy in contemplation of the blessed hope does not depend on your being rich, or well fed, warm or well clothed, appreciated, respected, or any of that. Christians who long for this blessed hope do so with a desire that is strengthened by hardship in this world. You may have come into misery in this world in any number of ways, but if the way you have come to ruin is through your addiction, you can have the blessed hope of the children of God this instant. You need to confess to God that you are in misery because of the self-gratifying way in which you have lived in rebellion against Him. Receive His forgiveness and lay hold of the blessed hope toward which you will persevere in this fallen world for the rest of your life. The fact that there is a great sense of anticipation involved in waiting for the blessed hope brings more motivation.

So what is this blessed hope? This blessed hope is the moment when the great Jesus bursts upon this world to take His own people to be with Him in His kingly splendour forever (Titus 2:13). What will His coming be like? It will be like the coming of a hero to rescue you when you are trapped in agony, about to die. It will be deeply emotional because the Rescuer has come to save you personally. His rescue has cost

Him dearly, to the point of being crushed to death under the most atrocious torture. From His heroic body, His lifeblood has poured compelling liquid beauty. As passionate as was His first coming in agony and blood, with loud cries and tears, forcing His way through tearing opposition, so will be the passion of His second coming. The eternal hero of God—the great warrior Jesus Christ—the suffering servant—will blast through the veneer of this sick, insulting world and free His dear people from the mangled wreckage of sin. This rescue will be dramatic beyond anything this world has ever seen. It will be jealously focused on His own. It will be visible and magnificent in the fullest sense. Because Christians are waiting for a Person, we have motivation that is personal.

Beyond all of this is the fact that the coming of the Lord Jesus, our blessed hope, will be marked by glory (Titus 2:13). The only word that will come to mind when Christ appears is "Glory!" Language restricts us from conveying the weight of the glory of Christ's coming. What will assault the eyes and senses of every person who sees Him on that day will be the unbearable splendour and brightness. The sun is likely the brightest light most people have ever seen, but on that day, the sun will be like a spark, drowned by effulgent glory.

Christ's brightness will be saying something. It will shout out His magnificence, excellence, dignity, and grace. You will suddenly realize that you are in the presence of a supreme ruler who emanates an atmosphere of absolute perfection, majesty, and deity. His sheer presence breathes unfathomable wealth and unassailable power. At His coming, Christ will be far removed from the man who died in shame on the cross, yet at the same time, He is exactly the same Christ. In His hands and feet, still visible, will be the marks of the nails that pierced His surrendered flesh, bleeding compelling liquid beauty. The fact that this glorious God bled for the likes of us will be too terrifying for us to contemplate at His return.

To the children for whom He died, the thought will be one of wonderful, staggering grace, but to those who by their rebellion continually nail Him to that cross, it will be the most frightening thought conceivable. His enemies will filter like ash to the floor in the blazing glory of His presence. This is the glory of Jesus. This is the glory of God, one and the same. And as God's people gaze upon this glory, they shall be transformed by it and clothed with it forever. Their God came into this world for them once as a sacrifice for their sins and has returned to take them home. They will be completely removed to unspeakable resplendence without end. The very thought of mundane life being swallowed up into this glory is staggeringly motivating.

What will happen to God's people then? Scripture uses an extravagant word to describe what happens next. The people for whom Christ will return will be his own special possession. They will be His very own. The Greek word used here (Titus 2:14) speaks of something that a person owns over and above the things he needs for ordinary expenses. It speaks of something that he owns as his own special possession that nobody can interfere with. It speaks of something, like a person's jewels that he keeps in a very safe place so that no-one else can gain access to them. It is something that the person has especially selected for his own use. Even in his own household, he keeps it aside for himself alone. It is something he treasures because it is special, unique, distinctive—one-of-a-kind. In fact, in non-biblical usage it spoke of being rich or wealthy, as having more than enough.

Can you grasp the concept that the glorious God of whom we have just spoken would hold His people in His hand in this way? They are jealously guarded from everyone for His own personal enjoyment, treasured beyond and above all He owns in His measureless treasury. Don't take this to mean that human beings are that valuable. We are not. Take this to make you appreciate the blessing God is going to lavish upon His people in spite of our worthlessness and rebellion. That speaks of the glory of God. It is a stupendous thought that God would jealously guard His people, close to Himself, as His very own special treasure. The intimate, personal nature of Christ's intentions toward His people is reason for unparalleled motivation.

So you hold onto this page in this present age, and as you read these words, the clock is ticking. You are waiting. Time is going by, and the return of Christ rushes toward you like the blast of an explosion. Valuable time is slipping by. What are you going to do with it? As the final moments before the great Savior's return thunder away, how are you going to live? How are you going to conduct yourself, so that when He appears you will be ready? God has instructions for you on this as well. The fact that God has given clear instruction in His word is cause for motivation.

What you have seen in Christ at His first coming, deliberately bleeding and dying for you, and in His second coming, returning in a glorious way to take you for Himself, are the teachers that will teach you how to live in the moments you have left. They will teach you to live by example. What you have seen in Christ is your example. They will teach you in the same way that a parent teaches his child, with persistent counsel and punishment. It is absolutely crucial that you take what you read here seriously.

What you will be doing while you wait for the blessed hope is working on personal purity in preparation for Christ's return. God has gone to these lengths to purify you. The fact that God has gone to such extremes to extricate you from your personal sin is extremely motivational.

The Bible gives us a term that includes everything we have been considering in this chapter. What we have seen in Christ is the grace of God. You can see the grace of God in His kind intentions toward His people before He even spoke the word and created the world. You can see the grace of God in the fact that He even created the world and human life at all. You can see the grace of God in the way He refused to destroy this universe when we, in Adam, rebelled against Him. We can see the grace of God in the way He withheld the full blow of His wrath toward rebelling human beings and reserved some degree of pleasure in this life for us. We can see the grace of God in overlooking the sins of His people before the time of Christ. We can see the grace of God in the way He has spoken to us over the millennia by giving us His Word, the Bible. We can see the grace of God in His coming into this world as a man, being hated, rejected, and murdered in order to rescue His people throughout history. We see the grace of God in changing people's hearts completely, making them into children of God by His Holy Spirit. We can see the grace of God in His persistence with His people through years of sinfulness as they progress in personal holiness. We can see the grace of God in His glorious return. We can see the grace of God in the way He will glorify His people so that they will be like Him. We can see the grace of God in freeing His people from sin in all of its forms forever.

Your heart can't beat without your experiencing the grace of God. You can't blink your eyes without missing something of the grace of God. The angels Isaiah saw said, "Holy, holy, holy is the LORD Almighty; the whole earth is full of his glory." The glory of God fills the earth, and one of the things included in God's glory is His grace. To miss the grace of God is like missing the water when you are at the bottom of the pool. It is impossible for a believer to live without seeing and studying the grace of God. Become a student of the grace of God. There you will find incomparable motivation.

Don't miss this point. It is as you search for, notice, study, meditate on, and desire to see more of the grace of God in His relation to people that you become aware of the contrast between the wonderful rightness of God and His grace and the ugliness, filthiness, and undesirable-ness of sin. You come to see sin's true colors. In fact, Paul says here that you come to see sin as such a grotesque thing in the light of the delightfulness of the grace of God that you develop a sharp resistance to sin (Titus 2:11). It becomes something hateful that you don't want to touch, like a maggot-infested carcass (chapter ten). This is God's design for you, by which you will pursue personal holiness. You will so intensely search out the thrilling grace of God that when the ugly suggestion of sin appears, you will immediately be filled with such holy violence that you will shout, "No!" in its face. Often, if you are anything like me, this shout will not just be a shout in your mind, but an actual, vocal shout that will thunder with all the hatred you have for sin in your heart because it takes you away from Christ. It takes you away from the grace of God into a grimy little cave of self-gratification that leaves you riddled with shame, guilt and regret. You don't want to go there again.

You want to remain under the white, shining purity of Christ which is of true value.

Paul shows how such a believer desires to deal with sin. He uses an interesting word. You do with your sin the same thing you do to a person with whom you have had a relationship in the past, but you refuse to associate with them anymore because you are ashamed of their conduct. You come to see the true shamefulness of your own private sins and refuse to be associated with them anymore. You want to be rid of them because they are so obscene in the presence of the dazzling grace of God. It is by devoting yourself to these things that you will learn to overcome your lusts for sinful pleasure. By gaining a clearer perspective of the grace of God, you automatically begin to hate sin more. This is thrilling motivation.

There is an interesting use of the same word (saying no, or denying) in 2 Timothy 3:5, that should be noted. Here Paul shows that there are people who actually deny the fact that there is any power in the Christian life at all. They see it just as another gimmick, another social club, or another religion. This is a very grave perspective. Perhaps it is your position too. Such people come under serious condemnation.

Specifically, by the authority of God's Word, it is by this powerful motivation we have just discussed that you will be able to put an end to habitual ungodliness, worldly passions, and wickedness (Titus 2:11, 14). Are these not the exact things from which you long to be free?

You may have been waiting for God to take away your desire for your addiction, but He hasn't. It should be quite clear by now that this is not the way God works. In the Bible, it is your personal responsibility as a child of God, to put to death by the

Spirit the misdeeds of your body (Romans 8:13). There is no better place to start than on the issue of ungodliness.

It is through comprehending the grace of God that you are taught to deny, and to say, "No!" to ungodliness. (Here I am emphasising the process involved in being taught, especially in the area of ungodliness). Ungodliness may not be one of the first things you would admit to because God may be very much on your mind as you struggle with your addiction under a load of guilt. To be ungodly is not to fail to think about God or to be unaware of His existence. It is to show lack of reverence for God in spite of all you know about Him. To be ungodly is to show that although you do know that you owe God worship and service, you just don't care enough to do it. You haven't made God's desires a matter of compelling force in your heart by dwelling on them and becoming driven by them. They hold little value in your personal agenda. To continue to live an ungodly life is to insult God's eternal grace. To suddenly realize that you could be classed as "ungodly," introduces a new powerful motivation toward godliness.

You will notice that it is the grace of God that teaches you to say, "No!" to ungodliness. (Here I am emphasising what the process involved in being taught is like). This word, "teaches" (*paideuô*), is the word you would normally use when speaking about the disciplined training of children. It involves both directive counsel and also punishment for doing wrong. Being a parent, I am moved by the suffering my children have to endure as they learn to be people of character. There is a lot of God-centerd counsel, a lot of failure, and a lot of punishment. It takes copious amounts of persistent, painful punishment for children to learn to do what is right. It is exactly the same issue in the Christian life. You must persist in developing godliness against your own fallen desires; therefore, Fatherly discipline must take place in your life. The fact that this teaching process will be thorough and will not take final failure as an option provides you with satisfying motivation.

The Bible isn't unrealistic when it comes to your personal struggle to control your desires. It understands that there will be a lot of suffering involved in the building of godly character, and it is when you are confronted with this pain that you so often fail. It seems too hard. Let me encourage you, as does 1 Corinthians 10:13, that every Christian does ultimately go through this school successfully. It is God who completes the work He has started in your life and He will make you holy whatever it takes. So the first thing a rich comprehension of the grace of God does is teach you to say, "No!" when you struggle against the urge to live in such a way that it is obvious that you have no respect for God—ungodliness. You demonstrate ungodliness in your failure to cultivate a relationship with Him in daily communion with Him and refuse to respect Him by simply structuring your life and desires according to what He desires rather than what you desire. The fact that God understands this trend in your heart and is prepared to see you through your struggle is reason for motivation.

Your comprehension of the grace of God also teaches you to say, "No!" to worldly passions. Worldly passions are those desires in your heart that drive you to live as if this world system is all there is and that God is absent. Worldly passions are desires that you harbor in your heart that set you in a position of hostility toward God because you desire things He has said are wrong. You are reaching out your hand to take things God has said you may not have, like the man who reached into the harvesting machine when he thought it was safe and got his arm mangled.

Worldly desires are lusts in your heart that you think about and dwell upon. They are identified by the fact that just the thought of gratifying them brings you pleasure, but the thought of not having them gratified brings you pain. Worldly desires are desires that focus on your own personal satisfaction regardless of whether it is achieved in a right or wrong way. Having suffered under your personal addiction, you are surely familiar with the desires raging in your heart. Again, I give you a word of overwhelming hope. God is saying in Titus 2:11-12 that through grasping the true wonder of the grace of God, even you will be able, by the empowering grace of the Holy Spirit, to gain control over those worldly desires. Comprehend the compelling liquid beauty. The fact that your most secret lusts are no secret to God, and that in spite of them He is still willing to power you through, that is massive motivation.

Even in this moment, you can lay hold of this hope by confessing to the Lord that you truly have lived with a knowledge of Him, but you have not lived as if you respect Him—maybe only an outward show for other people to see. Confess that the real master of your life has been your own personal desires rather than God and His excellent desires. Ask Him to forgive you and to drive you on with force by His Holy Spirit to develop godliness and godly desires that you will pursue. The fact that you have nothing standing in your way and that change can begin in your life this instant is hugely motivating.

Paul continues to show that even self-control is possible for you if you are a child of God. Self-control is one of the facets of the Fruit of the Spirit. You cultivate it, and the Spirit causes it to grow (Galatians 5:22-23). The self-control we are considering here is the sober-mindedness we spoke about in the previous chapter. Some people tell me about the way they struggle with self-control. They say that the moment the temptation hits them, they are overwhelmed and are unable to resist it at all. The first thing you need to give attention to if you are going to develop any self-control at all as a Christian is to deliberately search out a personal understanding of the grace of God. See the compelling liquid beauty of God, the blood of Christ that teaches you to control yourself. Before you laugh this off, remember that this is the teaching of God's Word. To laugh this off is to exhibit ungodliness, of which we spoke a moment ago. To simply believe this, accepting it as a child as the instruction of God, is to take your first step away from ungodliness and worldly passions and towards self-control and uprightness.

Truth is not relative. Truth is what God calls true. There is one final standard of what is right and wrong and that standard is what God has said in the Bible. To be upright is to acknowledge God's standard of truth to be the final standard for your life. To be upright is to insist that you will calibrate your evaluation of what is right and what is wrong by what God says is right and wrong. It is through exposing yourself regularly and constantly to the grace of God in Scripture that you will learn (be taught) uprightness. The fact that you have the very words of God in the Bible from which to learn appreciation for the grace of God is motivating.

I would like to close this chapter by pointing out something that should be obvious by now. Learning to live a godly, upright, self-controlled life is not a harsh, negative duty you pursue with a deep sigh. Living by the grace of God is not a heavy burden

God has laid on you, but something that frees you from slavery forever. To pursue self-control with your eyes fixed on God's compelling liquid beauty is to live with more passion than you have ever lived before. It is to be overwhelmed with desire to do what is right. It is a deeply personal thing. You know and love a Person who has loved you more deeply than anyone else in the entire world could ever love you.

Your devotion to Him is in response to both His giving of Himself for you as a sacrifice for your sin, and the grace He will still pour out on you forever and ever. God has desires in His heart for you which, if you could see them, would fire you up with passionate zeal for godliness and self-control. Through yearning for and coming to appreciate the grace of God more and more deeply, you begin to see these thrilling desires in the heart of God. The fact that God desires a satisfying personal relationship with you, rather than a morbid, ritualistic, slavery is dramatically motivating.

May I make an appeal? If you perceive the grace of God, and are still not motivated to live a godly life, you are in grave danger. If God's dramatic, universal display of love toward you doesn't move you to respond in similar, self-sacrificing love, the nature of your heart is glaringly obvious. I urge you to come to God in repentance, confessing this loveless-ness toward Him. Confess that you are not moved to respond to Him in love in spite of His blood and agony for you. Confess that your personal desires move you more than His grace moves you. Tell Him that you are unable to control yourself and are helplessly trapped in the grip of sin and hostility toward Him. Know that even from this state, the grace of God is able to rescue you in the most glorious way. When God has displayed His grace in saving a person like you, how wonderful will His grace appear to every eye in His glorious kingdom forever and ever? Is God's grace not simply too compelling and motivating to resist?

Chapter 14

PERSISTING
IN HOLY VIOLENCE

DR. EDWARD WELCH has such an excellent chapter on this issue in his book, *Addictions: A Banquet in the Grave* (chapter eleven)[35], that I would like to channel some of his content here. It is this same content for which I am indebted to him in the series I have preached repeatedly entitled, "The Exhausted Addict." Welch's chapter is named, "Staying Violent." I will put before you here some substantive issues he identifies. These are truths that will embolden you to stand your ground in the face of the onslaught of your personal temptations and sins.

In chapter eleven, I wrote about the twenty-five policemen whose eyes were so disported by the dancing girls that they were diverted from the mission that placed them in the club in the first place. Their mission was not to indulge themselves, but to enforce the law. They needed to remain resolute. They had a mission to accomplish. You also have a mission to accomplish, and you will need to be armed with a holy violence and insistence on doing what is right in order to put your personal damning sins to death. Here you will find truths that will reignite your fire for personal holiness again and again. Refer back to them, often, and walk in the strength they provide by the grace of God.

My dear brother Wayne, who is now living in the presence of God, taught me a powerful lesson on progressing violently in personal holiness. After many years of miserable addiction to drugs, the Lord reached into his life and brought about a transformation. I praise God for the fact that there are people who remember Wayne as he progressed violently in personal holiness after the Lord radically snatched him from the jaws of eternal misery. There are those who saw him struggle on and on, day after day, in the holy war. There are those who saw his selfless giving of himself and his belongings. There are those who saw him preaching the gospel both by his life and from the pulpit. There are those who came to know and love Wayne as a man with passion for the Lord Jesus, a man of power. In complete contrast to what he once was, the Lord made out of Wayne a man of God.

I mention this because Wayne is a real-life example of God's salvation from addiction. As you begin to move forward in your struggle as Wayne did, keep the following truth he learned in your mind. After the Lord changed his life, he worked hard among addicts, bringing them God's solutions. There is one thing he would tell me—one thing he truly desired to see in the lives of the addicts among whom he worked. He would say that he wasn't looking for people who were flying high above temptation but for people who were determined by the grace of God to *engage in the battle*. Constantly remind yourself to engage in the battle. With that word of encouragement, let's move on to the principles that will form the backbone of this chapter and your future war against personal sin.

Remember—You Are in a War

John Piper, in his book *Desiring God* said, "You cannot know what prayer is for until you know that life is war." If you read Edward Welch's chapter on this, you will find a gripping description of wartime. Every moment is critical. Every snap of a twig around you forces your senses to super-alertness. Your life depends on quickly identifying the enemy and reacting more quickly than he does. People who are genuinely holy are clothed with a type of aggression, a type of holy violence that erupts the instant a damning sinful desire surfaces. The enemy must be put to death—annihilated before it can covertly infiltrate and launch its massacre.

Welch says,

> There is a mean streak to authentic self-control. Underneath what seems to be the placid demeanour of those who are not ruled by their desires is *the heart of a warrior*. Self-control is not for the timid. When we want to grow in it, *not only do we nurture an exuberance for Jesus Christ, we also demand of ourselves a hatred for sin.*[36]

Of the many texts in Scripture that describe the war-like environment in which a Christian lives,[37] Wayne's favorite was Matthew 11:12. "From the days of John the Baptist until now, the kingdom of heaven has been forcefully advancing, and forceful men lay hold of it." The KJV reads, "...and the violent take it by force." This text paints a very graphic picture of the warlike attitude you are going to have to embrace as you engage

UNENDING HOPE FOR THE EXHAUSTED ADDICT

in the conflagration with your lusts. This is what it is going to take in order for you to be free from your damning addiction. This is the kind of lifestyle you are going to have to begin to cultivate. You have no alternative. It is only such people, who are absolutely desperate for God and absolutely desperate to be free from sin, who will finally lay hold of the kingdom of God. Remember, you are in a war.

Remember—Take Ground Progressively

You will notice that in Exodus 3:7-8, that although God had already given His people the Promised Land, they still had to fight for it and take the ground progressively. It is exactly the same with God's people today. No Scripture, in my opinion, speaks more eloquently on this issue than Romans 8:12-14. Paul says,

> Therefore, brothers, we have an *obligation*—but it is not to the sinful nature, to live according to it. For if you live according to the sinful nature, you will die; but if by the Spirit *you put to death* the misdeeds of the body, *you will live*, because those who are *led* by the Spirit of God are sons of God.[38]

Far from speaking about some kind of mystical leading by the Holy Spirit, what this text is teaching is that the people who are truly motivated, moved, driven, compelled, and forced into the violence of personal holiness are the people who are truly children of God. It is with this holy violence that you advance from one conquest to the next. Don't expect to destroy the hold of every sin over you immediately—rather, engage in the battle and be content to slaughter one personal lust at a time. Even then, deal with each lust progressively.

It is clear, again from Israel's conquests, that not every battle will be won. Don't give up at one or even multiple defeats, but be driven forward by the power of the Holy Spirit. Advance forcefully again and again. Remember to take ground progressively.

Remember—the Battle is Constantly Changing

This point is complimentary to the previous one. One of the most discouraging discoveries about fighting your personal sins is to wake up every morning and face the same old battle all over again. All you can see is the carnage of defeat after defeat. In fact, it seems to you as if you are in a unique situation and that you will never be free from your particular sin. I encourage you not to collapse into the trap of seeing the battle as the same old struggle every day. I say that because the battle is changing every day. It is never the same.

Remember Candi (chapter one) and how she got into the mess she found herself in? She descended into sin, step by step. It was as if she was descending a stairway down into a deep gorge. At every point she was on a different step. You have descended into your present state in the same way—step by step, decision by decision, concession by concession. Now, with holy violence, in dependence on God to empower you, you must begin the long journey back, one step at a time, one decision at a time, one denial at a time. Every time you take a step, although you are still in the gorge, you are not on the same step you were on previously. You have a different battle to fight, a different struggle to contend with. Regardless of all the similarities you see from day to day, there are many differences, and this alone should give you hope to continue. If you are engaging in the battle, you are moving forward and upward.

151

On Tuesday, you didn't have the experience of failure and renewal of holy violence you learned on Wednesday. On Thursday, you stood taller in the struggle, not only because you were nearer to the end, but because you had the added benefit of the lessons you learned from Wednesday's struggles. Look for the elements that make today's struggle different and take hope in them. Take note of the benefits you have accrued from past failure, from renewed dependence upon the Lord, and from renewed vigour in holy violence. Praise God you are on a different step to the one you were on before. Tomorrow you will again be on a different step. As a child of God, you will progress in violent holiness because God will most certainly be honored in your life.

You will find this teaching in Ephesians 4:19 and Romans 6:19. One lust satisfied shouts, "More!" Every step down into sin begs for another. The yearning drags you down, step by step. By the grace of God, resolve today to begin the journey back up out of personal sin to personal holiness. As a perfect booklet to help you do this, I highly recommend Dr. Jay E. Adams's, *Godliness through Discipline*.[39] Remember, the battle is constantly changing.

Remember—Sin is No Longer Your Master

The glorious truth is that God's children are set free from sin, and it can no longer dominate them habitually and permanently. Paul clearly says this in Romans 6:18, "You have been set free from sin and have become slaves to righteousness." This is a *fact* that is true of you if you have been saved. If your sins have been paid for by Christ and you are dressed in His righteousness, God has made you into a person over whom sin can have no lasting power. By God's grace you have the power and are obligated to throw off its controlling demands. You can fight this battle knowing that you will most definitely win. Admittedly, you may not win the first time or many times, but you will attain personal holiness in this area of your life as you grasp for it progressively, persistently, and violently.

You should also know that no temptation must inevitably lead to sin. Paul addresses this issue in 1 Corinthians 10:13. You will be tempted, and you will face difficult situations where your resolve toward violent personal holiness will be tested. These temptations will only be found in a limited array of shapes and sizes. In fact, you will never face a temptation that someone else has not faced before you, and overcome. You do have both the power and the resources to overcome your present struggle.

I know this because God is faithful, and He will not let you be tempted beyond what you can bear—says God. He knows you completely. He knows your situation completely. He knows the difficulties He will allow you to bear completely. Not one difficulty, says God, will be too much for you personally to bear in your circumstances. If you know that from the start, you should be bursting with hope. You will most certainly overcome this sin because God, with the difficulty, provides you with the power you need to stand up under it. Lay hold of this truth as another weapon in the war. Remember, sin is no longer your master.

Remember—Satan Is Defeated

As you discipline yourself in violent holiness, you are equipping yourself in the best possible way against the attacks of the devil. He has stretched his mind to its furthest reaches to develop a sinful environment in which you are most likely to be tempted. His propaganda is everywhere. You can't turn on the radio, surf the net, flick through a magazine, or walk the streets without being blasted by his sinner-seeking missiles. You struggle with porn? He has virtually naked women plastered all over the world and the media, all intent on seduction. You struggle with drugs? There is a whole system of agents with one hand out for your money, body, and soul, and the other hand clutching the chemical for which you yearn. You struggle with alcohol? Drinking is glorified to opulent status, and you are gunned down with the argument that it is acceptable to drink because it is social. He lulls you into oblivion by assuring you that you are a champion as you imbibe, doing the best you can to win. He guarantees you that anyone else in your shoes would do exactly the same as you are doing.

No! Don't give the devil's world system a chance to define your values, feed your lusts, or drag you away from Christ and eternal glory. Satan is defeated, and his presently powerful and alluring system will soon be destroyed forever. What will remain is what is of true value—God, His values, His people, His glory, His satisfying presence forever. You, as a child of God, stand in this present world system, fighting against its seduction by the power of God (Ephesians 6:10). As you give yourself to the simple Christian faith in increasing measure, you are doing the best thing possible to enable you to stand fully dressed in the armor of God in this hostile environment (v11ff). James says (4:7), "Submit yourselves, then, to God. Resist the devil, and he will flee from you." Lay hold of the certainty in that verse.

Satan now stands condemned before God. This present age, before Christ's return, is his opportunity to do the worst he can do. He is to be hurled into the ravenous jaws of damnation forever, never to trouble God's people again. Christ defeated him forever at the cross (John 16:11, Revelation 20:10). Your best defence against Satan is the violent pursuit of personal holiness. Remember, Satan is defeated.

Remember—You Are Not Condemned

You stand by grace (Romans 5:2). If Christ has died in your place and you are clothed with the righteousness of Christ, you are fitted to stand in the presence of God, forever delighting the heart of God. This is true because God is delighted in Jesus, in whose righteousness you are dressed. One of the accuser's favorite lines of attack is to drive you to think that you can earn God's favor by doing good things. You think that because you haven't smoked a joint or looked at porn this week, or even today, you are in God's "good books." Satan drives people to exhaustion in this way. He shouts, "More bricks! More bricks!"[40] You work yourself to burnout because you don't understand that in the eyes of God, you stand as perfect as Christ.

In your Christian life, you don't pursue personal holiness with violence because you need to earn God's favor. No! You already have God's favor. You can see what God did for you in Jesus on the cross. That is God's statement of passion for your salvation. God is satisfied with Christ's perfect life as a man.

The reason you pursue personal holiness with violence is because you desire to be holy as Christ is holy. You respond to God in love by pursuing personal holiness. This urge for personal holiness marks the life of every true believer because God the Holy Spirit lives in him. The continual yearning for personal holiness is not something you respond to in order to please

God. It is because God is pleased with you already that you have that yearning in the first place. If you are a true child of God, you long to be holy, and you feel you have no option but to pursue personal holiness with violence, you are not condemned (Romans 8:1). You are under God's grace, not under His wrath. You will never again face his wrath. Don't be incapacitated by hopelessness. Remember, you are not condemned.

Remember—Show No Mercy to Sinful Desires

One of the most powerful ways in which to progress violently in personal holiness is to study your sins and the ways in which you tend to fall into them. Take note of the people in whose company you sin; the place in which you sin; the things with which you sin; the circumstances in which you sin; the movies, magazines, websites, music, etc. around which you sin. Note everything about your sins. Look out for patterns. Every time you go away on a business trip, you tend to drink. Every time you speak on the phone with a certain person, you feel discouraged and sin. Every time you listen to a particular type of music or a specific song, you long for sinful sexual gratification. Take note of these things.

Once you have noted the environment in which you are most prone to fall into your favorite sin, remind yourself to be on the lookout for these circumstances, because it is in these circumstances that you are most prone to sin. See the whole cycle of sin as a chain. Your temptation begins with a very weak link—the phone call, the aroma, the sight of something that triggers fond romantic longings for your sin. It then progresses to a temptation, a stronger link, then a sin, a stronger link. As soon as you have identified the very beginning of the chain that draws you into your sin, learn to ruthlessly smash that chain without mercy. When the very first thought of sin enters your mind, destroy it with excessive force. Never allow yourself to pamper and flirt with the first link of the chain. Identify it and annihilate it. Take control of your body and the desires you experience in connection with it like Paul did in 1 Corinthians 9:27. He said, "No, I beat my body and make it my slave..." He did this in order to be qualified for the prize—a crown that will last forever.

Cultivate a disciplined lifestyle in small things and be vigilant in your war. In this way, the enemy is hindered from sneaking into your camp in the guise of a seemingly harmless entertainment. Remember, show mercy to sinful desires.

Remember—Fight with Hope

How often have I felt in my battle against personal sin, like a boy in combat with a giant. It is critical that you arm yourself with the attitude David had as he faced Goliath. Before he even engaged in the struggle he declared, "...the battle is the LORD's..." (1 Samuel 17:47). He was absolutely sure of victory before he even began to fight. Jesus Christ has already won the battle for you. You cannot earn what Christ has already earned. If you are a child of God—evidenced by a continual engagement in the war for personal holiness—you cannot ever be lost. You have already won eternal glory through Christ.

The **worst** thing you can do when you feel the desire to sin coming on is to feel the aggressive giant-like force and power of the temptation and immediately assume you have lost this fight. Don't do that. John MacArthur told the story of a construction worker working on a very high steel structure. He was working late so he was alone. He slipped and fell but managed to catch onto the beam upon which he had been standing, by his fingers. He couldn't hold on forever, and his grip began to slip. He was in distress, and with no-one to help him he was about to fall to his death—alone. He couldn't even send a last message to his dear family. Eventually, as the hour-like seconds ticked away, he gave up trying to hang on and plummeted. He dropped down the vertical surface of the building, approximately the length of his body, into a hoist-box. Was he relieved! The point is, when it seems that the temptation is so strong and there is no way out of it, don't believe the lie. Don't simply believe that because you are being tempted with such formidable force that you must sin.

Rather than simply hanging on by your fingernails (one of Wayne's favorite expressions), come to delight in your inevitable victory. Remember, fight with hope.

Here is one last story to illustrate my point.

Every year, my brother Kevin, being a concrete technologist, would build a concrete canoe and enter the concrete canoe race. Every year he lost the race. In my brother Wayne's final year before being received into eternal glory, he joined Kevin at the canoe race. Wayne was an extremely passionate man with a very athletic and muscular build—he kept himself in good shape. Kevin knew that if Wayne was going to be rowing, he would have to supply extra strong oars.

Eventually, the two of them were seated in the concrete canoe, anticipating the start of the race. Kevin reports that at the moment the starting gun was fired, he felt the boat lurch forward with Wayne's determined strokes. He was amazed at the power Wayne was putting into those oars. As they raced toward the buoy, Kevin began to feel fatigued but was amazed at how Wayne just continued to propel the boat forcefully forward, stroke after stroke. He was like a machine that couldn't be stopped. They rounded the buoy and entered the home stretch. Wayne was in such a determined mindset he hadn't even looked around to see the competition. Suddenly, as they approached the finish line, he looked around to see how they were doing. They had a huge lead. No-one could touch them now. Overwhelmed with excitement, Wayne shouted to Kevin, "Hey Kev, we're winning this thing!"

Even today I struggle to think of this story without strong emotions. Kevin was completely aware that it wasn't *they* who were winning the race. It was he (Wayne) who was winning the race. When Kevin's strength was depleted, Wayne just kept blasting forward and won the race for them. Kevin felt more like a passenger than a competitor. As you grow weary in your struggle against sin and have concluded that all is lost, don't down your oars and allow yourself to drift on the waters of sin. Christ is in your boat. He is pushing you toward eternal glory with more force than you could summon, even if you were given eternity to train. Remember, fight with hope.

I delight in the God of hope who pressed Wayne into this violent pursuit of personal holiness. May He graciously press you into this state of war so that your life begins to shine with the luster of Christlike glory.

Chapter 15

ASYLUM

IN THE INFERNO

SOUTHERN AFRICA IS the worst place in the world for grass fires. Every year we lose more to fire than does any other area. We who live on farms are all equipped with fire-fighting equipment. Particularly popular is a type of machine that consists of a 500-800 liter water tank attached to a high-pressure pump that runs off a lawnmower engine. Whenever it is needed, farmers can simply slip the empty unit onto the back of a small truck or onto a trailer behind a tractor, fill the tank with water, and go out to extinguish the fire.

Every year, many people die in the fires in South Africa. This year alone (2007) more than twenty people have died in fires. One incident that took place not far from my home a few years ago still lies heavily on my mind. A man and his wife were travelling along a narrow sand-road in their bakkie (SUV) following a fire, which was being driven away from them by the wind. They were towing a trailer loaded with a fire-fighting machine.

Suddenly, the wind changed direction, and the fire began to come directly toward them. The man driving the vehicle panicked and tried to manoeuvre out of the path of the fire. He pulled off too quickly and the fire-fighting machine slipped off the back of the trailer, jamming it in such a way that his vehicle could no longer move. There they were, immobile, in the path of the ravening flames. In their panic, they resolved that the best thing to do would be to jump out of the vehicle and run away from the flames, which they did. Sadly, as they fled across the grassland for their lives, the fire rapidly swept over them and burnt them both to death.

Family members who came to find them, found the couple's vehicle where they had abandoned it. They found the two bodies in the blackened field. How lamentable it was for these family members who examined this scene to discover that the vehicle was untouched by the fire. If the couple had simply remained inside the vehicle, they would still have been alive today. If they had simply stayed in that safe place, that asylum, they would not have been consumed by the inferno.

Your addiction is like that blazing fire. It desires to gloat over your charred body while you could have been safe inside the vehicle God has designed for your safety. So many addicts are so outspoken about the church today. They call it a gathering of hypocrites, irrelevant, unrealistic, boring, out of touch, and all kinds of other insulting terms. Sadly, many churches have pulled these kinds of insults down upon their own heads. Yet the truth remains that the church of Christ is still the only place where a true believer can find true support. It is the only God-designed environment where an addict can have all of the people around him that God says he needs in order to experience genuine, lasting change.

You come sprinting through the unburned grass, exhausted and terrified. Behind you roll the ravenous flames of a world of miseries that have come to you as a consequence of your addiction. You have been governed by your own desires and lusts and have not even considered God's desires for you. They have not featured at all. Your habit has been so consuming that nothing else in the world matters but that you gratify that yearning. No-one else matters regardless of whether they are standing in your way or are attempting to help you. Your overarching plan, direction, and intention is to satisfy your urgent cravings. How out of place do the requirements of God appear to you? You cannot think of anything less binding on you than God and His standards. You have tattered relationships with everyone around you and a non-existent relationship with God. You have no peace, no rest, only a relentless screaming in your head to stumble forward to the beckoning voice of your lusts.

You have lost out on so much in life. You don't know what it is to have a mature, self-sacrificial relationship with someone else, and you don't know what it is to submit to any kind of authority unless it is a pseudo-submission as a means to get something greater you desire. You have run into horrible consequences, and the only way you can escape the misery is to medicate it away, drink it away, or escape into the arms of your lover.

The following is a short e-mail written by a woman to her best friend Frankie. After he had used and deserted her, this was her appeal to him, as published in a local magazine. I have included it because it describes so well the state you may be in as you chase your addiction.

Frankie, you're throwing your life away; your beautiful thing.

Frankie, please read this. This is to my best friend, Frankie. I'm so hurt that you've chosen your "evil friend" cocaine above our special friendship. I've tried to help you, to support and love you but you choose your evil friend. Will he be there for you when you're feeling down, feed you when you're hungry, or love you when you're unloved? Will he listen to you when you need to talk? You have so much potential, so much love to give, so many wonderful friends—and you just don't care. I find that heartbreaking. I see people around me—needy, hungry, jobless people, and lonely people who'd thrive and rejoice if they had what you have. It makes me realize you don't appreciate anything in life. Life is a precious gift and you should cherish every moment, but you take it for granted. Maybe one day you'll realize what you had but it will be too late. I can't stand by and watch you kill yourself. Thank you for the precious moments we shared and the wonderful friendship we embraced. I'll never forget you. Your beautiful thing.

It is evident that there is only one thing in Frankie's life—coke. Coke is his god. His life is characterised by the fact that he is a coke addict. It affects every facet of his life. Nothing is left unstained. This is his identity.

If you have been reading this book and have confessed your sins to God and have received His forgiveness—if you have been saved—then the thing you need to understand is that you have a new identity. You were once a selfish sinner, like Frankie, charging ahead of the greedy flames with sure death snorting down your neck, but now you have become a member of the household of God (Ephesians 2:19-20, 1 Timothy 3:15). You have been adopted into God's family (Ephesians 1:5). You are now part of a whole new race—a chosen people, a royal priesthood, a holy nation, a people belonging to God (1 Peter 2:9).

For too long you have lounged around with the name, "dope addict," or "heroin junkie," or "alkie," stamped in your identity document. Once you have been granted the grace of membership in God's family, you now become, "child of God," "servant of the God of heaven," "united with Christ," or any of the many new titles of those received mercifully by God into His household. Put an end to your old identity. Throw it into the flames where it belongs and enter into the asylum—the place of safety—the church where you will find others who answer to the same titles. You are now a child of God, not a junkie. Junkies hang out with junkies. Children of God hang out with children of God. Junkies pursue their lusts to their death. Children of God pursue the desires of God whether it means life or death. Deliberately take on this new identity and associate yourself with the people of God rather than with the people who are similar to you merely in the kind of sin in which they indulge. You no longer have anything in common with them but have everything in common with the other members of God's household.

More than anywhere else in the entire world, you will find real help in the church. With time you will come to appreciate the vast spectrum of people God has called into fellowship with Himself, from spectacularly varied walks of life. The day will come when you, having grown in personal holiness, will be confronted with a young convert, fresh out of a drugging lifestyle, and he will wonder how such a gathering of people—so clean and smart—can help him. You will be able to look at him with compassion, smile, and offer him genuine, lasting help.

You would be surprised to hear the stories of those in the church. More than that, you would be surprised to see how such vastly different people can live together in such harmony. In one church where I was a member, there was the contrast between one man who was a pharmacist, sitting beside another who had been a Spitfire pilot in World War II. If God has saved you, your place in the body of Christ is reserved and you must come in and serve.

Choose a church that is devoted to the apostles teaching, that is God-centerd, and that shows a loving concern for the needs of people.[41] In such a church you will not be left to live by your own best guesses and motivation, you will be under the wise leadership of men who have walked a significant way on the road to personal holiness (Hebrews 13:17). They have faced many of the gruelling battles you are facing and will still face.

For the first time you will be able to learn a way of life where you will come to experience the true and satisfying role of a man or woman in God's design. You will be called upon to serve in the body of Christ in the capacity for which you are suited, and you will find joy in your work. For the first time you will find that life has meaning. You will see the godly examples of other men and women and be amazed by the way in which the Lord has blessed and preserved them regardless of what they have had to live through.

You will come to desire godly character and will be motivated to work toward it. You will learn to contribute to the true corporate worship of God, worship flowing from a heart that is enthralled with Him. You will take your place among the number gathered together, so you can serve with delight. Instead of taking everything you can get your hands on, you will come to thrill in giving cheerfully to the Lord as much as you are able to give. You will find that God has given you personally the ability to serve in the body of Christ in a special way. In the use of your gift, you will also find joy.

You will find brothers and sisters in Christ who will love you enough to care for you. You will find people to whom you can be accountable, and they will desire to help you. They will be bold enough to confront you in your sin and bring you back into the blessings of a close relationship with the Lord and those in the body of Christ. You will find that the entire focus of the members of the church is toward others, not themselves. Each member will serve the other in love, and in that way delight the heart of God. You will find that you have the privilege, for the first time, to feast in direct communion with God with a clear conscience and a pure heart. You will also be able to pour out your heart to God for other brothers and sisters in Christ because you care for them deeply as you see them struggling under the scourge of sin as well.

You will have new power to pray for the entire church of God so that she will stay strong and be able to bring great honor to God in this dark world, holding up the truth, holding up a God-focus, holding up care for each other. Before you have devoted yourself fully to rewarding church life, you will not be able to understand properly what it is all about. What you used to call unrealistic, you will find to be the most real thing in the universe. What you used to call irrelevant, you will find to be the most relevant thing in the world. What you used to call boring, you will find to be the most thrilling, motivating, purifying, and exhilarating thing you have ever experienced. Welcome to the family of God.

Edward Welch also shows that it is the body of Christ that helps you remember. It helps you remember that God and His glory are the most important things in this world and in your life. To addicts, the most important things in the world seem to be not getting caught, avoiding pain, having independence, or whatever it is that is on the top of their agenda. This will change. The body of Christ helps you to remember that your greatest need is to worship God, displaying true humanity at its peak, as did the Lord Jesus. The church helps you remember the reality of God's grace and life-changing power as you see Him changing other people as well. It helps you remember, as you look around you in the roaring flames, that the church is the only asylum in the inferno. This should not only motivate you to entrust yourself to the church of God, but to serve others who have sinned in the same way you have sinned.

The church helps you remember that every church can be critiqued by any addict. There can often be serious problems in any local church. The church is filled with saved sinners. They are fallen. They fail. And they sin. This should make you feel right at home. They are very much like you. The church helps you to remember that you are not saved by your own performance, but by the grace of God.

If you are ever going to change in such a way that your change is acceptable to God, it is going to take place within the asylum in the inferno—the church. It is only there that you will find everything you need because the church has been perfectly designed by God for that specific purpose. The flames will devour every person who attempts to run to safety, by his own technique, while those in the asylum will be preserved before the face of God.

I conclude with a quote from Welch,

In our battle with sin, *we need a team of people.* We need teachers to help us understand Scripture, prophets to help us apply it, interceders to pray for us, preachers to focus our eyes on Christ, encouragers to remind us of God's grace when we feel like failures, wise men and women to discern when we are making foolish decisions, and people of faith to tell us that everything God has said is true in Christ.[42]

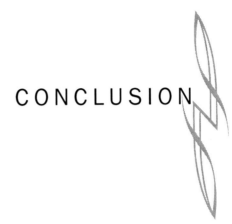

CONCLUSION

TO BUILD UPON the illustration I used in the previous chapter, just like the people running into the burning grass, you are *inclined*, like Candi, to run out onto dangerous ground rather than running for the safety of the vehicle—the church—God's asylum in the inferno. Out of the millions of voices screaming at you, telling you what to do, only one can be trusted, the voice of God in the Bible.

Even though you are being burned by the consequences of your sin as a victim, you continue to sin voluntarily, proving yourself a violator as well. God is pushing you, through your misery, to repent.

Further, you have deceived yourself into thinking that your addiction is not obvious to people around you, it is a secret thing. But life becomes overwhelmingly burdensome and painful, and your hope lies in your being confronted with your sin, so you can be convicted and repent. Not tears that come from circumstantial misery—tears that come from realising that you are offending God.

In the face of your glaringly real struggles, you have genuinely believed in your heart that Jesus is too weak, tame, and domesticated to snatch you from your misery. God is calling you to personal devotion to Christ in the same way as Christ is personally devoted to the will of His Father—passionately.

You may even be staring at God's solution to your problem, but you are so deceived by sin that you don't perceive your obvious personal need for a Savior or the danger you are in.

God is not pretending He doesn't know that there is a degree of pleasure in sin. The pleasure you experience is the reason why you do it. Rather, He desires you to control yourself by His grace, for this short stretch of time on earth, so you can delight in a dazzling eternal inheritance that dwarfs the delights of sin. Where is your attention?

If you are a believer, there are many ways in which you can arm yourself for battle so that you can overcome the forces of sinful deception that drag you into the pleasure of your sin. This kind of life is possible and commanded for the believer in the Lord Jesus Christ.

The only place in which you can expect to see genuine, lasting change in your life is within the family of God, the church. The church has been designed by God to have everything you need to change from being a self-centerd sinner to being a man or woman who delights the heart of God.

May God, by His grace, draw you into this wonderful new life of delight and certain success.

APPENDIX

A S I HAVE worked with people addicted to substances and sinful habits, I have learned many things. Below are a few things I have labored over, that you as an addict, or you as a person who desires to help an addict, may find helpful.

I Have Learned that the Addict Is Broken

On 1 February 2007, I received the following e-mail:

Good day Alan,
I tried to phone but I can not seem to get through on your landline (lot of static). Is it possible for you to give me a bit more info. on your program? I know a young man of twenty-five that has difficulty seeing the bigger picture, dwelling around in life with no future. We have tried everything and a lot of rehabilitation centers later, he is still not going anywhere in his life. (Heroin addiction, cannabis, street drugs, alcohol. He could have been involved with Satanism on one point as well).

His family does not want him living with them anymore due to the fact that he always makes promises and never keeps them, can't hold a steady job for long, and keeps on falling into darkness every time. He has consulted with psychologists a few times, taking meds for depression and more.

He needs something more out of life and it does not seem that he is listening when his loved ones talk to him about doing his own thing and looking out for himself. (The family keeps on giving and he knows this.)

Will he finds his way back if he commits himself to Grace Manor's Sanctuary for a year, if you can help him, what would the cost be? This is an urgent request, and I am awaiting your reply soonest.

Thanking you in advance…

For a while, drugs really seem to be helpful and under control. After a while, negative effects begin to show up. Master becomes slave. Life begins to change in the following ways (lists such as these are well documented in almost any book on drug addiction).

- Addicts become restless and struggle to sleep.
- They suffer from fatigue and increasing irritation.
- Even the smallest things are too much for them to bear.
- They often feel drowsy and experience unexplainable mood swings.
- They will do strange things such as migrating to another group of friends, leaving good friends behind.

- They will begin to spend less time with their family and more time with their new friends, often dressing to identify with their group.
- They become very touchy about their privacy and complain when they suspect people are prying into their affairs.
- When people who love them try to help them, their help is intentionally misinterpreted as intrusion.
- They seem to lose their respect for people they have always respected before and throw off restraint.
- They do increasingly irresponsible things.
- In those who are studying, there is often a decline in academic achievement.
- People who once had high moral values now seem to be throwing them off, involving themselves in things they would never have involved themselves in before.
- Their personal hygiene begins to decline, and they begin to become sickly.
- They become dishonest, and eventually they don't even bother to hide it.
- They lie, manipulate, and avoid eye-contact.
- They sell their personal belongings and those of others for ludicrously small sums of money.
- Their eating habits change, and they begin to lose weight.
- They avoid spiritual talk and spiritual activity.
- They begin to talk about suicide and the activity of the devil.
- They begin to steal things from around the house, including money.

- They develop a sudden interest in things like pornography or pharmaceuticals.
- Co-ordination problems become apparent, coupled with delayed reactions, slurred speech, and mild to consuming anxiety and panic.
- They struggle to remember and become excessively aggressive especially when their drug use and alcohol consumption coincide.
- Their sex drive declines and they begin to talk a lot—unnaturally.
- They sleep far more than they used to or need to.
- They seem to have outstanding energy or stamina at times and then at other times exhibit exactly the opposite.
- They lose their ability to reason.
- They begin to cover up their tracks by burning incense, wearing dark glasses, using eye drops, or eating strong-smelling foods.

Volumes have been written on the way in which drugs and alcohol affect people's bodies and their ability to think normally. My point in this is to mark the misery of the addict who comes for counselling. They are often broken and cry uncontrollably. They have run out of resources. Some have so ruined their brains that they will never be able to pursue a course of study in order to qualify in any significant line of work. They have destroyed friendships with friends they should have cherished. They have sold all of the personal belongings they ever had. The money is all used up (thrown into the incinerator and now they need more). They have destroyed their relationships with their parents (whatever good they had). They have made themselves unwelcome in their family home and even in the homes of their drugging friends. They have resorted to things they never thought they would resort to in order to fuel their hellish master screaming in their ears—stealing, mugging people, dealing in illegal drugs and trafficking, prostitution, or sex slavery.

Now where do you start with this broken mess? Let me suggest something that may sound shocking—you begin as a student. You sit there to learn. This is a hard lesson I have had to learn as I have worked with broken people. You can learn from them. I have fallen into the trap of thinking that because I have devoted myself to learning how to counsel from Scripture, that I am qualified to advise counselees who sit before me, then shout, "Next!" Oh, that God would grant us the eyes to see and the ears to hear the screams of agony, the fear and anguish gushing from the hearts of these wasted human beings who are being torn away into the endless wretchedness of Hell. Oh, that you and I would approach these broken people with the heart and passion of Jesus Christ.

The Lord has been pleased to humble me through my dealings with addicts. Even though it was never my intention to appear aloof in counselling, that must have been the way in which I came across on occasions. Only after a number of counselling sessions did the people in question point this out to me. Considering the grievous fact that I have this potential within me, my mind has spent some time considering a specific portion of Scripture.

Read Job 12:1-5, Job's first application of sarcasm. The moment has come for him to deal with these people who have come to counsel him. Although there are many dissimilarities between Job's case and the case of the exhausted and broken addict, one major similarity is in how these counsellors dealt with a man who really was experiencing disaster, ruin, and calamity. Everything was gone, and it had a crushing effect upon him.

Although there seems to be some difficulty in understanding the Hebrew in this particular verse for translation purposes, there is wide consensus as to Job's intended meaning. I quote from the *New American Commentary*.

> The versions all differ on wording but seem to mean the same thing, that is, that Zophar and his friends could afford to be smug because they were rich and healthy.[43]

In fact, we may even read this text to include the thought that when a person falls into ruin, the thing that naturally happens (a result) is that he attracts contemptuous counsellors.

When dealing with someone who is struggling, like the addict, what strikes you immediately is their lack of understanding in many things. They have a small, subjective, self-centered world and don't grasp the vast objective world of theology you do. Don't let those observations lead you to the contemptuous reductionism that Job's "counsellors" were reduced to as they confronted him in his misery.

Consider your personal failures when travelling, when going through difficulty, and when becoming weary. Consider living a whole life like that, but instead of coming back to the Lord, confessing, and receiving His forgiveness, you go on to abandon Him. You become consumed by your own selfish agenda (imagine the horror of your personal sins overwhelming you—as they have obviously overwhelmed the individual before you). Consider the relationships you cherish the most being violated and smashed so no-one wants to be around you anymore. Imagine everything you have worked for and value, snatched away—like Job, sitting on the ground in the ashes, surrounded by ruin and misery, scraping his sores with a piece of broken pottery. Imagine the terror of being in a wrong relationship with God because you are trapped in a sin from which you are powerless to escape. As much as you long to be in a right relationship with God, you simply can't break the chains that hold you.

Before you speak, consider the fact that the addict's life really is miserable. Without grasping this and allowing it to deeply affect the way in which you deal with him or her, you will pull down upon yourself the insults that Job's friends earned. If you don't set your heart to listen to what this person is saying—as if you are hearing this kind of misery for the first time in your life—and allow the tragedy of his "lost-ness" to heavily sway your way of dealing with him, he will immediately write you off as unable to help. You are too comfortable to help, too rich to help, too educated to help. You don't understand.

The addict's pain lingers, and it is in his pain that you must counsel him. It is in his pain that he needs to be evangelized, convicted, taught and set up straight again (2 Timothy 3:15-16). It is in his pain that he must repent. This is exactly what Job experienced in Job 16:4-6—the pain remains. You are speaking to a person in pain.

I Have Learned that the Addict Is Proud

There is something else that I have not been able to avoid as I have dealt with addicts. You are looking into the eyes of a person who is ruined and broken and miserable with seemingly no fight left in him. He seems to fit the picture of Psalm 51:17—broken, contrite, someone the Lord will not despise. He is so broken that, without any pressure, he can break down and cry to the Lord from the depths of his heart. He can pray with the kind of depth and sorrow that many believers have never even experienced.

Naturally, your heart goes out to him, and you long to help him. You already have some portions of Scripture in mind that you will unfold with the new sense of urgency for his soul that is brewing in your heart. But as you take hold of this soft clay in your hands and begin to nurse him to health with the Word, something else emerges. Two things appear that seem to be contradictory and mutually exclusive. At the same time that the exhausted addict is broken, he is often proud and unteachable. I have had difficulty dealing with this because it is hard to understand how a person can be so broken and so proud at the same time.

One of the first ways in which this pride manifests itself (and any person who has attempted to help an addict must have heard this before) is when the counselee lays his presupposition on the table. He asks you if you have ever been an addict. When you say no, he immediately loses respect for you. He then considers himself to have the upper hand, and his relationship with you, in his mind, turns from being student to teacher. This stumbling block in counselling used to discourage me, and I thought about it a lot.

One day, as I was reading Romans 3:16-17, it dawned upon me that the reason the addict's life is marked by ruin and misery is because he doesn't know the way of peace. The next time I found myself in that situation; I heard the low blow coming and was ready. I asked him who he would rather go to for lessons on something, an expert or someone who knows nothing. Of course he replied with the expert—thinking I was going to say that a person who has had a drugging past is the expert who is best able to help him. I said, that by God's grace, there was something God had taught me that I would like to teach him. What was that? It was *the way of peace.* I then explained that the fact that he was sitting here before me and the fact that his life was in a state of ruin and misery were clear demonstrations (biblically) of the fact that he didn't know the way of peace. I approached him on that basis, rather than on the basis of being a drug expert—which I am not.

As I looked into what the Bible has to say about pride, something very significant emerged. Let me share this finding with you.

Two significant words in the New Testament that are used side by side paint the picture for us. The one is *huperephanos* (hoop·er·ay·fan·os), and the other is a*lazon.*

Huperephanos, translated *arrogant* in Romans 1:30, means to show oneself above others, over topping, to be conspicuous above others, or to be pre-eminent. Second, it is to have an overweening estimate of one's means or merits, despising others or even treating them with contempt, being haughty.[44]

Alazon, translated *boastful* in Romans 1:30, means to be an empty pretender, a boaster. *Alazon* describes the person who boasts about possessions and abilities he doesn't actually have.[45] Its antonym is *tapeinós,* which speaks of a person who is humble, who places himself on the ground floor.[46]

In both Romans 1:30 and 2 Timothy 3:2, the term *alazon* is set directly alongside the term *huperephanos* and seems to be almost equivalent.[47]

What is more striking than the actual definitions of these words, especially those found in Romans 1, is the context in which they are found. The *Theological Dictionary of the New Testament* shows that *alazon* portrays the corruption of idolatrous paganism.[48]

Romans 1 portrays the unredeemed masses under the wrath of God (v18).

They have rejected God—an evidence of their pride (verses 18 and 21 are examples).

They have chosen God's "things" rather than God Himself (verse 23 is an example). Judas is illustrative of this. God is on the one side, the handful of coins on the other. They have used God's things in the wrong way. Sex is abused (verse 24) and perverted (verse 26-27).

They are pursuing a paradise where all of their lusts can be grouped together in one perfect environment, but in contrast, they are ending up in the miserable consequences of their sins—the wrath of God. Consider again the list of consequences and unpleasant side effects (above) that follow the addict around.

Paul continues in Romans 1:29 by saying, "Furthermore…" and then goes on to list other manifestations of sinfulness with which the idolater is seasoned. It is among the words in that list that we find *alazon* (boastful) and *huperephanos* (arrogant).

Is the sinful nature not bizarre in its tenacity? Here is a man who is perpetually putting his hand out to take hold of things God has told him not to touch. He is like the man of whom we spoke, who put his hand into the harvesting machine and got it mangled. He is both reaping the temporal consequences of his sins that are ruining him, making him miserable, and breaking him, and he is also facing the eternal wrath of God. Still he has an attitude about him that he is above everybody else. He has an air of superiority from which he looks down upon all the people around him. It is as if you came to help that man jammed in the machine, only to have him tell you that he doesn't need your help. He is quite qualified to extricate himself.

And so it is that this mystery is resolved. This is what the Lord says the idolatrous heart is like. You face a broken addict. Yet at the same time you face a proud addict. So how do you go about speaking to a person who is weeping in lament but who is simultaneously defying you as a person and as a representative of God? I think the answer is found in 1 Timothy 4:12. Here Paul says,

> Don't let anyone look down on you because you are young,
> but set an example for the believers in speech, in life, in love,
> in faith and in purity.

Regardless of whether you are young or not, the principle stands.

The transaction works both ways. Remember, I showed in the first point that the addict is broken. And as Job suggests, a broken person tends to call contempt upon themselves by their condition. We also said that the greatest danger from the very start of counselling is to respond to the temptation to look down on the broken addict in that situation. Don't consider yourself educated and organized and, as such, above the person whose life is in a mess. Don't be as proud and arrogant as he is.

But at the same time, Paul instructs Timothy not to let anyone look down upon him because he is young. The solution he gives Timothy, the method of dealing with a person who looks down on him, is to live such an exemplary life that people will respect him for his way of life. So, as you pursue a humble approach, refusing to act in a learned and arrogant way, you are showing the example of a life that will put an end to the person's reason to look down on you from his proud position. Don't put fuel on his fire of arrogance and boastfulness by competing with him for prominence.

I Have Learned that the Addict Is Miserable

Although I have already said something about the addict's misery in my first point, there is more, and it has practical value.

When studying 2 Timothy 3, we come across a group of words in verses 2c-3 that include words that describe interpersonal relationships within the family. It reads,

> People will be lovers of themselves, lovers of money, boastful, proud, abusive, disobedient to their parents, ungrateful, unholy, without love, unforgiving, slanderous, without self-control, brutal, not lovers of the good...

Read the text with emphasis on *disobedient to their parents.* Consider the others: ungrateful (*acharistos*), unholy ("*anosios*—without consecration—no regard of duty to God or man" *Complete Word Study Dictionary NT)*, unloving (*astorgos*), irreconcilable (*aspondos*), etc.

As in the e-mail with which I began this appendix, one thing you will notice about the addict is that he has left a trail of ruined relationships behind him. And very often, he can't name one person who would be happy to see him on their doorstep. In my experience, addicts are unwanted. They have engineered this condition for themselves by their conduct among other people.

There is one word among the group that has stood out with particular force. It is the word, *astorgos*—without family love. Like some of the other words in the group, it is a word that describes a strong positive virtue that one would *expect* to find in a particular environment, but it is then negated with the "a" that precedes it. As in the case of *astorgos*, Paul is speaking of *family love*. What is interesting to note is that by God's common grace, even in unbelieving families we still often see family love. But in the last days we will see children growing up who will be without family love. They will be sons and daughters, brothers and sisters, mothers and fathers, who will not love each other.

Consider the thought the Lord puts forward in Isaiah 49:15.

> Can a mother forget the baby at her breast
> and have no compassion on the child she has borne?
> Though she may forget,
> I will not forget you.

It is unthinkable, when thinking according to God's perspective, that a mother could forget and have no compassion on the child to whom she has given birth and is feeding. The bond between that mother and child is tight and close. But today it is not uncommon for a woman to give birth to a child and to throw her own child into a rubbish bin. We know that this kind of thing has happened, to a degree, throughout history. My point is that this is not normal. What is normal in God's world by God's common grace is that mothers love their children; fathers love their children; children love their parents and each other. But that is all going. *Astorgos* will increasingly mark the generations in our times.

Consider the child born and raised by a caring mother. The most natural thing in the world (as we have seen from Isaiah 49:15) is that the child, as soon as he is able to understand what is going on, will look at his mother and love her. But Paul is describing another kind of transaction where a child who should naturally be expected to love his parents, who have nurtured him for so many years, will fail to love them. He will fail to obey them. He will fail to show or even feel any sense of gratitude. He will fail to acknowledge any authority over him. He will determine his own direction in life regardless of the most basic obligations to his family. He has no family love.

The reason I make so much of this is because this is the condition in which you counsel an addict. He comes to you broken, yet proud, asking for help but extending himself for no-one. I focus on this because this is an excellent point of contact with such a person. The very reason he is sitting before you is because he has so destroyed everyone and everything of value around him that he is now completely out of resources. He can proceed no further because his tank is empty.

From what I hear, he wants you to listen to his life story, and instead of you remarking on his disobedience to his parents, his ingratitude, his unholiness, his lack of family love, his refusal to be reconciled with his parents, other people, and God, he wants you to hear his story and remark on how heroically he has managed to get through this whole ordeal so undamaged. The pride we have been speaking about fishes for compliments by telling long stories that are designed to make you confess, "If I was in the situation you are in, I would have crumbled. I would never have been nearly as strong as you have been."

As I listen to the life this person has lived, my agenda is his repentance. I consider the way in which he has related to his own mother, father, brothers, and sisters. What he has said to them, how he has stolen from them, and even—as in the one case—how he threw his own mother to the floor and sat on top of her holding a knife to her throat. I show this person the connection between the misery he is in and his disobedient, ungrateful, unholy, loveless, irreconcilable life. Then, if appropriate, I turn to Psalm 32 and show the agony of the man who keeps silent and refuses to confess his sin. I then show the moment of release in the psalm, which comes with confession. This conviction of sin works best when the counsellor uses specific incidents in the counselee's life, using specific names, places, and things.

I have also had the opportunity to speak to addicts whom the Lord has convicted of sin and who live with a sense of wonder at what the Lord has done in their lives. When I asked the one man about the scar on his face, he told me the story about how he had been involved in gang activity. There was a fight. At one point an opponent had picked up a brick and hit him in the face with it. He said that that was the moment he began to think seriously about life. In fact, after learning a new godly perspective on life, he said that he had been so insistent on having his own way that God had to hit him in the face with a brick to stop him.

I Have Learned that the Addict Needs Theology

There is nothing I know that has proved more beneficial and life changing to addicts than for them to come to understand something of a God-centerd world view. For years they have been at the center of their own world and no-one else has mattered. For them to be exposed to the agenda of God and to be shown where they fit in proves repeatedly to be life-changing.

It is through discussing the facets of theology with them that evangelism takes place. I like to bring the gospel to them through the different facets of theology. Some areas in theology that the Lord has used particularly powerfully in my dealings with addicts are listed below.

1. The doctrine of the Word. For most addicts, it is a new concept that the Word of God has authority over them. It has never occurred to them that they are not the final authority even in their own lives. God has spoken and His words are binding on them.

2. The doctrine of man. God created man in His own image. One man was devastated when I explained to him (a little further along in counselling) that God doesn't need mankind or the rest of creation for anything but has chosen that they will bring Him joy and glory. After a time of emotional re-adjustment, he embraced this teaching with such joy that it was the pivotal point in his life change. His whole demeanour changed.

3. The doctrine of sin. Many still feel they have the power to extricate themselves from their lifestyle regardless of the ruin and misery they have experienced. When they are shown their true helplessness before God, as I follow through with teaching on man's depravity, some are brought to their knees. When God opens their eyes to see their ruinous state, they repent.

4. The doctrines of grace. Their understanding of what is fair and not fair is completely overturned as they consider God's sovereign electing grace. Suddenly, their notion that they will come to God when they please is shattered,

and they become overwhelmed by the fact that their salvation doesn't depend on *their* word, spoken at *their* convenience. A desire for the mercy of God becomes clear, and their attitude changes visibly in other areas as well. The addict comes to the realisation that salvation is not like a tap that one turns on when he pleases. Rather, it is the gracious gift of God when He (God) chooses. As far as God's gracious work of salvation is concerned, this picture of grace can also be used as a contrast to his own personal graceless life. While God is gracious, the addict is hostile both to God and to other people (irreconcilable). Again, he will only come to grasp this contrast when God has already performed His saving work in their hearts. To teach the grace of God, however, is also a wonderful evangelistic approach.

5. Providence. God's outstanding wisdom. Use incidents in the counselee's life, such as the brick incident I used earlier, to help him see that this is the moment that God has brought him to. It is momentous, and God is presenting the truth to him right here and right now. He dare not take this opportunity lightly. The events of his life, though they may seem chaotic to him, are all carefully ordered and managed by God. God has brought the addict here. Right here and right now the Word of God places demands upon him to repent and to spend the rest of his life pursuing God's agenda for him, not his own. To listen carefully to the addict's life story and to show him the way in which God has brought him to this point, opens up a shocking awareness of the hand of God in his life when they were not even aware of it.

It makes a rebellious person feel small in contrast to the great God.

6. Progressive sanctification, ongoing confession, and forgiveness. Addicts become very discouraged when they fall again. I like to major on confession and forgiveness. They come to understand that the Christian life is not a matter of making a great resolution and, then, living it out. It is a matter of growing into Christ-likeness. It appears to me that people who have lived their lives in a very sinful way seem to be too hasty to rectify everything all at once. They set themselves unrealistic goals and thus experience repeated failure and discouragement. To teach progressive sanctification persistently is to help them to avoid this trap.

7. The teaching of future glory, beginning right now. I show the glory to which every believer is most definitely going. I then show that the life of delighting in the glory of God begins right here and now. Become what you are. I love John Piper's book, *Future Grace*. Its perspective has motivated me and helped me to motivate discouraged believers struggling with persistent sins.

I Have Learned that the Addict Talks Too Much

One of the areas in which I have had to be firm with addicts in counselling is that of talkativeness. I love to communicate and to communicate clearly and accurately. This often takes a number of carefully chosen words. The words you choose to speak carefully color the meaning you convey to another person. Having spoken about the way in which a sense of self-rule governs the addict, or any unrepentant sinner, I find myself compelled to make this final comment on how that autonomy is expressed in the words of the addict.

It was my father, years ago, who brought this thought to my mind, and it has been simmering since then in all of my contact with addicts. One of the things most commonly communicated by addicts is the misery they are in. This doesn't come across in a neutral way but is deeply stained with a dye of blame. There seems to be a relentless grasping in the addict's words for a suitable place to lay blame.

You may object and say that in your experience, addicts quite freely confess that it is only them who are to blame for their present misery. While I agree that addicts often do say that kind of thing, repeatedly, one would be wise to hear all of the other things they say in addition to those confessions. While they often lay the blame for their ruin at their own feet, their words continually probe, even into the lives of the people around them who love and care for them the most, for reasons to blame.

A wise counsellor will take note of all of the people and events addicts blame for their misery. He will then notice that the addict himself has excused himself from most of the blame. His own offences seem to be painted with a type of unsuspecting naïveté. Even though he may confess to some vile actions, those actions are presented in such a way that he appears quite reasonable, maybe even commendable, under the circumstances.

A text that speaks loudly and picturesquely on this issue is Romans 3:19. There Paul speaks of every mouth being silenced and the whole world being held accountable to God. In the mind's eye, one can almost hear the ear-splitting babble of voices, all speaking at the same time, all explaining, all making excuses, all justifying their habits. It escalates over the centuries, louder and louder, until God shouts indignantly for silence in His courtroom. The universe falls deathly still, moments beating intensely by. Everyone has finally stopped talking—blaming, accusing, protesting, complaining. This will be the final moment when everyone stops talking.

In the life of an addict, it doesn't have to be this way. He can come before God right now and stop talking. He can acknowledge that he stands before God, guilty as accused—fallen beyond repair and deserving of God's punishment. He can call out to God for mercy rather than giving an explanation, an excuse, or another justification.

I find it very helpful to simply listen to the addict and ascertain whether he is still *talking* or whether his mouth has been silenced before God. Does he see his grave condition with enough sobriety to realize there is nothing he can say to remedy this situation? His whole life he has been talking himself "out of a paper bag." He has been talking to deceive; talking to cover up; talking to regain the favor of people he has insulted by his lifestyle; talking to gain money, drugs, clothes, place to sleep. His whole life of addiction has been a long jabber. I see the first glimmer of hope for the exhausted addict when he stops talking in that defensive way and acknowledges his guilt before God.

Often, I speak to my father on counselling issues. We have a saying between us. When we are attempting to come to a conclusion on the state of an addict, my father simply asks me, "Has he stopped talking?" If my answer is no, he knows exactly what kind of difficulty we are sitting with.

This is a good final note upon which to end this appendix. It is an appeal to you as an addict to take note of the way in which you have become accustomed to speak. Take deliberate note of the way in which you convince yourself and others that you are quite innocent and that your sinful habits are the result of someone or something else's influence on you. You consider yourself to be in a position from which you cannot reasonably be expected to escape. Stop talking. Stop justifying. Stop arguing. Stop blaming. Stop manipulating with your words. Stand silent before God and confess that you are in a state of ruin because of the deliberate choices you have made and continue to make. Confess that you truly are lost, and ask Him for mercy. Ask Him to save you from your sin—sin that compels you to immeasurable ruin and misery. "…[Christ] is able to save *completely* those who come to God through him…" (Hebrews 7:25)[49].

Author's Contact Information

Websites: www.graceunlimited.co.za
www.sermonaudio.com/graceunlimited
E-mail: exhaustedaddict@graceunlimited.co.za

Postal Address: P.O. Box 1903
Bronkhorstspruit 1020
South Africa

BIBLIOGRAPHY

Adams, Dr. J.E. *A Theology of Christian Counselling*. Grand Rapids: Zondervan Publishing House, 1979.

Alden, R. L. *Job* (Electronic ed.) Logos Library System. *The New American Commentary*. Vol. 11. Broadman & Holman Publishers: Nashville, 2001.

Elwell, W. A., and Beitzel, B. J. *Baker Encyclopedia of the Bible*. Grand Rapids: Baker Book House, 1988.

Kittel, G., Friedrich, G., and Bromiley, G. W. ed. *Theological Dictionary of the New Testament*. (Electronic ed.) Translation of *Theologisches Worterbuch zum Neuen Testament*. Grand Rapids: W.B. Eerdmans, 1995.

Mack, Wayne A. and Swavely, Dave. *Life in the Father's House: A Member's Guide to the Local Church*. Phillipsburg, NJ: P&R Publishing, 2006.

Mans, Pieter. *Drugs: A Streetwise Guide: An ABC for Parents and Children*. Western Cape, South Africa: NDB (for Lux Verbi. BM) Lux Verbi 2000.

Mc Cafferty, C. *The Pink Agenda*, Cape Town: Christian Liberty Books, 2001.

Pitkin, Ronald comp. *Theological Dictionary of the New Testament*. Translation of *Theologisches Worterbuch zum Neuen Testament*. (Electronic ed.) Grand Rapids: W.B. Eerdmans, 1995.

Powlison, David *God's Love: Better Than Unconditional* P&R Publishing 2001

Ryken, L., Wilhoit, J., Longman, T., Duriez, C., Penney, D., and Reid, D. G. *Dictionary of Biblical Imagery* (Electronic ed.). Downers Grove, IL: InterVarsity Press, 2000.

Strong, J. *The Exhaustive Concordance of the Bible : Showing Every Word of the Text of the Common English Version of the Canonical Books, and Every Occurrence of Each Word in Regular Order* (Electronic ed.). Ontario: Woodside Bible Fellowship, 1996.

Tan, P. L. *Encyclopedia of 7700 Illustrations: A Treasury of Illustrations, Anecdotes, Facts and Quotations for Pastors, Teachers and Christian Workers*. Garland, TX: Bible Communications, 1996.

The Saturday Star newspaper, (South Africa) 11 March 2006, Edition 1, "Teen Sex Shock" by Noor-Jehan Yoro Badat

The Star newspaper (South Africa), 13 January 2004 Edition 1: Article "Titillation at Your Expense?" by Estelle Ellis

Welch, Dr. Edward. T. *Addictions: A Banquet in the Grave: Finding Hope in the Power of the Gospel*, Phillipsburg, NJ: P&R Publishing, 2001.

Zodhiates, S. *The Complete Word Study Dictionary: New Testament* (Electronic ed.) Chattanooga: AMG Publishers, 2000.

ENDNOTES

1. This account is a reconstructed version of a true story reported in *The Saturday Star* newspaper (South Africa) on 11 March 2006, Edition 1, "Teen Sex Shock" by Noor-Jehan Yoro Badat

2. All of these were mentioned in the *Saturday Star* article as the reasons why young people act in the way that Candi did. The name I have given her is, of course, fictitious.

3. Emphasis mine.

4. For more on this, consult Dr. J. E. Adams, *A Theology of Christian Counselling,* 108-118.

5. *The Saturday Star* newspaper (South Africa) 11 March 2006, Edition 1, "Teen Sex Shock" by Noor-Jehan Yoro Badat

6. Ryken, L., Wilhoit, J., Longman, T., Duriez, C., Penney, D., Reid, D. G. *Dictionary of Biblical Imagery,* 87.

7. Elwell, W. A., and Beitzel, B. J. *Baker Encyclopedia of the Bible.* Map on lining papers. 1,932.

8. Welch, E.T., *Addictions,* 12.

9. Emphasis mine.

10. Mc Cafferty, C., *The Pink Agenda,* 30 (Emphasis mine).

11. Emphasis mine.

12. Ephesians 4:19 (emphasis mine).

13. Emphasis mine.

14. I have taken these ideas and words from Welch, *Addictions*, 90-93.

15. Zodhiates, *The Complete Word Study Dictionary: New Testament* (electronic ed.) G5318.

16. Strong, *The Exhaustive Concordance of the Bible,* (electronic ed.) G1567.

17. For a consideration of this distinction see Adams, *A Theology of Christian Counselling,* 215.

18. *The Saturday Star* newspaper (South Africa) 11 March 2006, Edition 1, "Teen Sex Shock" by Noor-Jehan Yoro Badat

19. Available from www.timelesstexts.com. In fact, I have drawn the following argument from that particular book.

20. Also available from www.timelesstexts.com.

21. Even though this was an incident reported in a national newspaper, I have deliberately withheld names and places.

22. I have taken the idea of domestication from Dr. Edward Welch's book, *Addictions*, 143.

23. Powlison, David, *God's Love: Better Than Unconditional,* 14

24. The twenty-one-part series entitled, "The Passion of Christ," is available for free download from www.sermonaudio.com.

25. Although this event is based on a true story from a newspaper, I have deliberately withheld detailed information that would perpetuate the negative impact this event had on the persons involved.

26. *The Star* newspaper (South Africa), 13 January 2004 Edition 1: Article "Titillation at Your Expense?" by Estelle Ellis

27. *The Star* newspaper (South Africa), 13 January 2004 Edition 1: Article "Titillation at Your Expense?" by Estelle Ellis

28. Mans, Drugs: *A Streetwise Guide: An ABC for Parents and Children,* 54.

29. Tan, P. L. *Encyclopedia of 7700 illustrations : A treasury of illustrations, anecdotes, facts and quotations for pastors, teachers and*

Christian workers Illustration no. 1277 (electronic edition; no page number) I have filled the story out with fictitious details to make it more colorful—not, however, altering the list of stomach contents.

30. Although self-control is not mentioned in this particular text, notice that other facets of the Fruit of the Spirit are listed. Compared to Galatians 5:22-23, we can affirm that self-control is in view when Paul writes this verse. See also 1 Timothy 3:2.

31. See how self-control is expected of everyone, especially young men, in Titus 2:1-6.

32. Tan, P. L. *Encyclopedia of 7700 illustrations : A treasury of illustrations, anecdotes, facts and quotations for pastors, teachers and Christian workers* Illustration no. 845a (electronic edition; no page number)

33. Kittel, G., Friedrich, G., & Bromiley, G. W. *Theological dictionary of the New Testament,* 1150

34. This chapter is a study on Titus 2:11-14. I have deliberately kept the delivery of the material non-technical.

35. Welch, E.T. *Addictions,* 225-245

36. Welch, E.T. *Addictions,* 225

37. Examples are Ephesians 5:15-16; 6:11, 1 Peter 1:13; 2:11; 5:8, 2 Peter 1:5

38. Emphasis mine

39. Available from www.timelesstexts.com.

40. Imagery taken from Exodus 5.

41. Mack and Swavely, *Life in the Father's House,* 55.

42. Welch, *Addictions,* 252. (Emphasis mine)

43. Alden, *Job* (page 150 electronic ed.).

44. See Strong, *The Exhaustive Concordance of the Bible.* (electronic ed.) G5244.

45. See Strong, J. 1996. *The Exhaustive Concordance of the Bible.* (electronic ed.) G213.

46. Zodhiates, *The Complete Word Study Dictionary: New Testament* (electronic ed.) G213.

47. Friedrich, ed., *Theological Dictionary of the New Testament*. Vol. 10 Ronald Pitkin, comp. (electronic ed.) 1:227.

48. Friedrich, ed., *Theological Dictionary of the New Testament*. Vol. 10 Ronald Pitkin, comp. (electronic ed.) 8:527-529.

49. Emphasis mine

Printed in the United States
124276LV00002B/87/P